# FIFTY RELIGIOUS FILMS

## ALAN PAVELIN

Published by A.P.Pavelin, 172 Leesons Hill,
Chislehurst, Kent BR7 6QL


Printed by Printronics, 25 Shelton Street, Covent
Garden, London WC2H 9HT

ISBN 0 9516491 0 8

Front cover: still from Bresson's *Les Anges du Péché*
(courtesy of Electric Films)

Back cover: still from Pasolini's *The Gospel
According to St. Matthew* (courtesy of British Film
Institute)

# CONTENTS

# INTRODUCTION

Most people have a good idea of what is meant by a Western, a musical, a thriller, or a sci-fi movie. The same probably applies to the "religious film", a phrase which perhaps instinctively conjures up an image of Charlton Heston dividing the Red Sea, or of Jennifer Jones seeing visions at Lourdes.

A moment's thought, however, shows that it is not so simple. While the films covered in this book include some of the type just referred to, the Biblical blockbuster or the portrait of a saint, many good religious films are highly individualistic and far from what might be easily categorised.

Several of the films included are purely fictional, while still likely to be classed by most people as "religious". They tell stories, usually based on novels, about fictitious characters caught up in some spiritual situation or crisis, generally from a point of view which is either sympathetic or neutral towards the particular beliefs being portrayed.

Other films may not seem at face value to have much to do with religion, but can nevertheless be seen, and are intended to be seen, as Christian parables or allegories. Some of these can be enjoyed as dramas purely on the surface level, but they become more interesting when the deeper implications are recognised.

Some other films appear to have little or no religious reference, but are included because they reach to the very fundamentals of the human condition and to our life on earth, and can certainly evoke a religious response in the viewer. Because it requires great artistic skill to present such issues seriously and authentically, and in a way which evokes an appropriately reverent response, these films are often among the greatest ever made.

Finally, and possibly controversially, some films are included which might be classified as "anti-religious" in varying degrees, notably those made by Bergman and Buñuel. No apology is made for this; no mature person should, or even can, shield himself or herself from sincerely-held beliefs which may be uncongenial. As is pointed out in the course of the book, to attack religion is to pay it the compliment of being an important force in society and in people's lives, of being worthy to be taken very seriously.

So the films included are a wide selection under the broad category of "religious" in the ways described above. All are interesting, most are good, a few are among the greatest masterpieces of all cinema. The best are far more than just "filmed stories"; by having great attention paid to the style in which they are filmed, they can transmit spiritual truth and values just as great literature, painting, and music can. No claim is made that this selection represents the "50 best" of their kind, a claim which would imply that it is possible to give them an order of merit. The choice includes some which the writer knows and loves well, some which are great by anyone's standards, and some well-known "commercial" films which avoid the banalities of most modern Hollywood-style cinema.

Whilst I am a Christian believer, the book is not intended to be religiously polemical, and it is hoped that it will be of interest to those who, without necessarily being believers themselves, nevertheless regard the cinema as a legitimate medium for the exploration and transmission of spiritual ideas and values. In many cases, my own views on the issues raised by the films are briefly stated.

Of the films I have selected, six each were made by Ingmar Bergman and Robert Bresson, and five each by Roberto Rossellini and Andrei Tarkovsky; to a large extent this reflects my preferences among directors. The leading countries of production are

6

France (9), the USA (9), Italy (8), Sweden (7), and Britain (5). 31 of the films are foreign-language.

Specific reference has been made to "cinema", implying that a film which was made for the big screen, and is more than just light entertainment, should if possible be seen there. Briefly, the disadvantages of television or video as a means of watching a cinema film include the TV screen's size and shape (for which TV actors often try to compensate by ludicrous over-acting), the commercial breaks which can ruin the "flow" of a film, and the fact that British television shows films too fast, which may not matter except that music is played at the wrong pitch. Most fundamentally, television, with its domestic interruptions, is not conducive to the concentration which a really good film demands, and it is of interest that modern commercial movies have become rather like extended TV ads, complete with final freeze-frame of the hero looking happy and contented.

In practice most people in Britain, and nearly all outside London, seldom have the opportunity to see good films in the cinema, especially the older films like most of those discussed here. The big cinema chains, which seem to be run by the kind of people who know the price of everything and the value of nothing, cater largely for fans of adolescent junk-movies such as the pathetically witless "comedies" which seem to predominate, whereas people who would like to see a Robert Bresson film, for example, may well have to wait a lifetime. It is hoped that this book, on an aspect of cinema which has hitherto been largely neglected, will encourage an interest in some of the outstanding films described in its pages. It is also hoped that those with the power to determine what is made available for the public to see will allow such films an occasional airing, and not just in the few so-called "arthouses" to which most people do not have easy access.

## ANDREI RUBLEV
### Andrei Tarkovsky, USSR, 1966

Andrei Rublev, the greatest of Russian icon-painters, lived between about 1360 and 1430. In 1988 he was canonised by the Russian Orthodox Church as part of its millennial celebrations. Little factual material is known of him, but Tarkovsky, in his second feature film, created an imaginary and imaginitive reconstruction of seven episodes of his life, with such titles as "The Passion of Andrei" (including a vision of Calvary with Rublev as Christ) and "Last Judgement". At over three hours, and shot in the Soviet equivalent of Cinemascope, the film has established itself as an epic masterpiece.

Set between 1400 and 1423, the film is based on the premise that Rublev became so sickened by the violence and immorality of his times that he decided to give up painting and take a vow of silence (a theme which also appears in Tarkovsky's final masterpiece *The Sacrifice*). Then, at the end of the marvellous final episode entitled "The Bell" (which is virtually a little feature film on its own), Rublev is so moved by the faith and action of a young boy that he renounces these vows and embarks on his greatest work. The moment of renunciation is one of the most moving of all cinema, and is followed immediately by the eruption of this previously black-and-white film into glorious colour, as we see details from several of Rublev's greatest works including the *Trinity*, reproductions of which are often to be found in religious houses in the West.

The fact that the film is not historically accurate (there is no reason to suppose that Rublev actually made such vows) does not matter; poetic licence can surely extend to the cinema. What the director is doing is to demonstrate the tremendous power of faith in unleashing artistic creativity in the service of the Church.

Making full use of the wide screen (one reason why *Andrei Rublev* should be seen in the cinema if at all possible), Tarkovsky demonstrates the magnificent visual style for which he is famous: the natural elements of water, fire, mist and light which are such a feature of all his films, and the majestic use he makes of his favourite animal, the horse. The re-creation of 15th century Russia seems authentic as far as one can tell, with the Tatar invaders sweeping across the plain from the East to lay waste the city of Vladimir. The director makes admirable use of those marvellous long takes for which he is justly acclaimed, and which for me make his films so hypnotic.

The character of Rublev is played convincingly and sympathetically by Tarkovsky's favourite actor Anatoly Solinitsin, while the boy in the final episode, "The Bell", is portrayed by Nicholai Berdyaev who had starred so confidently in Tarkovsky's powerful earlier feature *Ivan's Childhood*. Acting ability is far more essential in films such as this, consisting largely of long-held shots, than in those made up of brief shots all neatly pasted together in the editing-room.

*Andrei Rublev* has other grounds for fame, quite apart from its supreme merits as a film: it was notoriously shelved for years by the Soviet authories, was not seen in the West until the 1970s, and has only relatively recently become available in the USSR itself under *glasnost*. One can only suppose that the authorities saw it as too sympathetic to religion, and they may also have objected to its scenes of violence and nudity, which are however neither gratuitous nor exploitative.

With scenes ranging from theological disputations to pitched battles, *Andrei Rublev* is a monumental work, a landmark in religious, Soviet, and world cinema.

# ANGES DU PÉCHÉ, LES
## Robert Bresson, France, 1943

Few directors have made as masterful a first
feature film as did the French Catholic, Robert
Bresson, with this spiritual drama set in a
Dominican convent dedicated to the welfare of women
ex-convicts. This is one of only two films in which
Bresson used professional actors; within a few years
he was to decide that amateurs, who were more likely
to do exactly as they were instructed and whom he
referred to as "models", better suited his purpose as
a film-maker.

*Les Anges du Péché* ("Angels of Sin", a
sensationalised title which Bresson did not choose)
is centered around two main characters, the young
upper-class novice nun Anne-Marie and the intrac-
table ex-prisoner Thérèse. At their first meeting in
the prison Anne-Marie decides that her divinely-
appointed destiny is to "save" Thérèse, whom she
invites to live at the convent on her release.
Unknown to the nun, however, Thérèse's first act on
leaving prison is to shoot dead the man who, she
claims, committed the crime for which she was
imprisoned. She understandably resists Anne-Marie's
personal crusade on her behalf, seeing the convent
merely as a place of refuge from the forces of the
law.

Thérèse's continual rejection of Anne-Marie's
passionate interest in her eventually causes a near-
nervous breakdown in the young nun, who becomes
angry and arrogant. Disciplined by her superiors,
she refuses to perform a penance and is asked to
leave, to Thérèse's private pleasure. When Anne-
Marie is found one night exhausted in the grounds,
having been praying at the grave of the order's
founder, she is re-admitted, and Thérèse is assigned
to nurse her. Anne-Marie is too weak to speak the
words of her final vows, and in a kind of spiritual
transference Thérèse speaks them for her. The young

nun dies, but the ex-convict has accepted respon-
sibility for her crime and gives herself up to the
police.

This somewhat melodramatic, thriller-like plot
is used by Bresson as a peg on which to hang the
underlying spiritual conflict which is his main
interest here. His noted austere style is already in
evidence, with much use of the close-up to show us
not so much the exterior appearance but the inner
state of the characters. The whiteness of the
convent scenes contrasts sharply with the dark of
the prison, with obvious theological symbolism; the
prison metaphor persistently recurs in his films
(*Les Anges du Péché* was made three years after
Bresson's own release from a Nazi prison camp).

One of the film's main themes is redemption,
not just of Thérèse but also of Anne-Marie. Both
are, in their own way, rebels, one the murderess and
the other the rather arrogant young nun whose
commitment to the vow of obedience leaves something
to be desired. Both find their redemption in the
moving scene at the end of the film, when they have,
as it were, exchanged personalities.

The film's theological thrust is very clearly
Catholic rather than Protestant. There is no
suggestion that Anne-Marie is "fighting the good
fight" against the authoritarianism of the religious
order; rather are its rituals and ceremonies
portrayed with the utmost respect and affection.
The spirit of convent life is admirably conveyed.

*Les Anges du Péché* can make a strong claim to
being the finest of all films set in a monastery or
convent. It is wholly serious in intent, and is
imbued with a powerful spirituality which is neither
sentimental nor jocular. Under Bresson's controlled
direction the acting, the script (by the noted
dramatist Jean Giraudoux), and the luminous black-
and-white photography are all splendid, and any rare
opportunity of seeing this film should not be
missed.

# AU HASARD, BALTHAZAR
## Robert Bresson, France, 1966

By the time of making *Au Hasard, Balthazar* Bresson's unique cinematic style was well-established: a pared-down austerity which allows nothing unnecessary to be seen or heard, the use of non-professional "models" instructed to avoid all rhetorical acting but to make wonderfully expressive movements of the eyes, and the swift cutting from scene to scene which often leaves the viewer to *infer* what is happening rather than having it spelt out. This style enables the actively-minded viewer to "see" below the surface into the characters' very souls. Anyone who tries to watch a Bresson film passively, as if it were light entertainment, will get nothing out of it.

The film can be seen as a Christian allegory. Balthazar is a donkey, and we follow his life from birth (almost) to death. This is interspersed with the life of the main human character, the girl Marie, who as a child is given the baby donkey as a companion for herself and her friend Jacques. As his life progresses Balthazar is put to work as a beast of burden, sold by Marie's father to a bakery where he is mistreated by the delivery boy and motor-cycle gang-leader Gérard, adopted by the tramp Arnold who uses him to give donkey-rides and then sells him to a circus, sold at auction to a cruel miller, rescued by Marie's father, and used by Gérard for smuggling. On one of these expeditions Balthazar is shot by a customs official and dies on a hillside surrounded by a flock of sheep.

As for Marie, her adolescent passion for Jacques ends when she is seduced by the selfish and aggressive Gérard; she later lives with the miller when she is rescued along with Balthazar, but finishes up being cruelly beaten by Gérard. She is last seen cowering naked in a corner, as Balthazar is going to his death.

There are many specific Christian references. Balthazar was supposedly the name of one of the wise men at the Nativity, while the donkey is traditionally wise as well as stupid. Marie can be identified, partly, with the Virgin Mary. As a child she baptises Balthazar in a stable and gives him the "salt of wisdom", and at one point her mother calls him a saint. Gérard seems to symbolise the Devil (he has no redeeming features at all), while Arnold, despite being an alcoholic, is in some ways a Christ-figure (he never retaliates against Gérard's taunts and cruelties, rides on an ass, and is given a kiss of death by the treacherous Gérard). Most memorable of all is the beautiful final scene of the innocent Balthazar with the sheep, a lamb very prominently in the frame. He has come full circle, because the first scene also includes a flock of sheep.

These references are not the central religious interest of the film; this is rather its fascinating meditation on free will, not just in a brief discussion by two minor characters but in the way the main characters are portrayed. Marie and Balthazar are both passive; the latter because he is an animal who cannot help himself being acted upon, the former because, although making choices, she is one of society's victims. Arnold also is passive; Bresson seems to be saying that a "sinful" act (Arnold's alcoholism) should be judged according to the degree of freedom possessed by the person committing it, a profound theological truth. On this criterion only Gérard falls under judgement. (In real life we cannot of course judge people in this way as we simply are not in possession of all the "facts", but in a film or a novel we are presented with all we need to know.)

*Au Hasard, Balthazar* is one of Bresson's best, most thought-provoking, and most moving works, a film from which one gains more at each subsequent viewing.

# BABETTE'S FEAST
## Gabriel Axel, Denmark, 1987

Despite being one of the the most popular foreign-language movies shown in London cinemas for many years, *Babette's Feast* was still not allowed a normal release in the suburban and small-town Odeons and Cannons. It seems that the big distributors simply do not want to expose their regular customers to having to read sub-titles, or to seeing a film, however enjoyable, which is rather more intelligent than the comic-strip nonsense which seems the staple fare of present-day Hollywood.

Based on a story by Isak Dinesen (Karen Blixen), better known for *Out of Africa*, the film tells of two elderly unmarried sisters, Martine and Filippa, in a remote 19th century Jutland village, keeping alive the memory of their clergyman father. They are devoted to asceticism and good works among the elderly and poor of the village.

In a flashback to when the sisters were young and beautiful, we see how Lorens, a young cavalry officer, was strongly attracted to Martine, but leaves in awe of her father and their piety. Shortly afterwards M.Papin, a French opera singer, is entranced by Filippa, but she calls off the blossoming relationship and he returns to France.

Years later a Frenchwoman turns up on the sisters' doorstep with a letter from M.Papin begging them to give her sanctuary from persecution in Paris. Babette turns out to be an excellent housekeeper and cook, but after several years' service she learns that she has won 10,000 francs in a lottery. This saddens the sisters, who expect her to leave, but instead Babette offers to spend her winnings on a lavish feast in celebration of their father's centenary, to be shared by all the members of the little religious community.

When the lavish provisions arrive the sisters are horrified, expecting some kind of orgy. The guests decide beforehand that they will refuse to enjoy the food, and will make no comment on it whatsoever. There is an additional guest, however: Lorens, returned to the village after many years tortured by the idea that he may have made the wrong decision in leaving Martine. He is amazed to discover that the food at Babette's feast is just like what he knew at a top Paris restaurant, but he elicits no response when he remarks on this to the other guests. The joy of the meal breaks down the reserve of the locals, and they forgive each other for past wrongs. Finally Babette reveals not just that her entire winnings were spent on the meal, but that she had indeed been the head cook at the Paris restaurant.

The religious truth which this delightful film conveys is that the things of this world can be both enjoyable and good, that food is a gift from God which can break down the barriers between people, that it is a kind of sacrament. There is a strong undercurrent of the conflict between the puritan Protestantism of Northern Europe, suspicious of any kind of sensual enjoyment, and Parisian Catholicism, regarded as "decadent" by this Lutheran sect. It is these fears which are overcome, suggesting a kind of conversion, not to Catholicism but to a less austere outlook in themselves. The film implies that this is a conversion for the better.

Another theme is the character of Babette, movingly portrayed by the French actress Stephane Audran. She makes the sacrifice of all her winnings, wishing only to proclaim herself as the "great artist" she once was, not in any boastful sense but in order to bring delight to people. She is portrayed as an almost saintly figure, in strong contrast to the locals with their petty squabbles. The meal itself is the centrepiece of the entire film, leaving the viewer with a thoroughly satisfying, if hunger-inducing, experience.

# BLACK NARCISSUS
## Michael Powell, GB, 1947

The famous Powell-Pressburger partnership was responsible for some of the most startingly original and imaginitive films in British cinema. *A Matter of Life and Death* for example, a fantasy which portrays heaven as a kind of gigantic sports arena, presents life on earth as perhaps a more desirable experience. *Black Narcissus*, despite having little to say on directly spiritual matters and being both exotic and erotic, is very firmly set in a religious environment. It is based on a novel by Rumer Godden.

A young Calcutta nun, Sister Clodagh, is appointed Superior of a new school/hospital high in the Himalayas, in the former palace of a rich Indian ruler who has given it over to the Order. We soon meet the bizarre mixture of characters in the area, including the Englishman Mr. Dean, always doing odd jobs around the place; the benefactor's nephew, the "young general", anxious to be educated among the classful of children; the local temptress, whom Mr. Dean installs in the convent to be rid of her; and the old "holy man", who seems to spend his entire life seated silently in the same position in the convent grounds, visited by the local villagers. The film's title refers to an exotic scent used by the young general.

This totally new environment, with such features as the distinctly unspiritual pictures on the walls, has a profound effect on the nuns. Several little incidents trigger off Sister Clodagh's memories of her one-time love for a young man who decided to go to America without her. The elderly nun recalls her early life after many years of not giving it a thought, and decides she has to leave the place. The emotionally unstable Sister Ruth develops a crush on Mr. Dean, and is consumed with jealousy to see him talking alone one evening with

Sister Clodagh. Another nun gets into trouble with the young Superior for covering the gardens with flowers instead of vegetables.

Things come to a head when Sister Ruth fails to renew her yearly vows, dons lipstick and a glamorous dress, and goes off to find Mr. Dean. That worldly but basically decent man insists that she return to the convent, where she picks a fight with Sister Clodagh at the edge of a high cliff with disastrous consequences for herself. This tragedy prompts the departure of the remaining nuns just as the rains begin, fulfilling Mr. Dean's prophecy that they would not last until the rainy season.

Visually the film is ravishingly beautiful and is shot in a highly stylised, somewhat artificial way with exotic colours and huge close-ups, of eyes or leaves. The Himalayas are reconstructed in the studio. The acting is somewhat theatrical but memorable, with Deborah Kerr as Sister Clodagh, Kathleen Byron as Sister Ruth, Flora Robson as the elderly nun, and Jean Simmons in the non-speaking rôle of the young Indian temptress. Miss Kerr convincingly portrays the underlying emotions and discomfort beneath her authoritative exterior.

The film's portrayal of the nun's sexual longings would be regarded by some, and was so regarded on its release, as sensationalist and offensive. There is a fine line to be drawn here. I would undoubtedly find offensive any portrayal which suggested that the religious life is purely and simply a substitute for a sexual life, and those who hold this view are either giving vein to their prejudices or extrapolating from their own personal experiences which may not apply to others. On the other hand it is certainly unwise to repress one's desires, to pretend that they do not exist, and this is what the nuns in *Black Narcissus* seem to be doing, with tragic results for one of them. This is generally understood today by the level-headed people who opt for the religious life.

# COLOUR OF POMEGRANATES, THE
## Sergei Paradjanov, USSR, 1969

This astonishing film from Soviet Armenia was banned for many years by the authorities, and the director was imprisoned. It emerged in the West in the late 1970s in a pirated copy shortened and drained of colour, and was not seen in its full glory until its eventual official release in 1983.

Steeped as it is in Armenian cultural tradition, the Western viewer cannot expect to make anything like complete sense of it but will undoubtedly marvel at the incredible colours and imagery, much of it religious, which fills it from beginning to end. It is loosely based on the life of an 18th century Armenian poet and monk called Arutiun Sayadian, better known as Sayat Nova (King of Song), who became an archbishop and died defending his cathedral from Moslem invaders. It is presented, however, in the highly unconventional form of a series of tableaux, with brilliantly-garbed groups of actors positioned in a highly stylised manner, as a voice-over reads extracts from Sayat Nova's poems and provides a commentary on the action.

Framed by a prologue and epilogue, there are eight "chapters" with titles like "The Poet's Childhood", "The Poet's Youth", "The Poet Becomes a Monk", and "The Poet's Death". Sayat Nova is portrayed at various stages of his life by three different actors and an actress, who is an identically-dressed female double, the Muse, who guides the poet into the world of fantasy, mystery and desire.

In the prologue, blood-red juice oozes out of three pomegranates and forms a stain in the shape of the original Armenia (part of which is now in Turkey), as the narrator intones "I am he whose soul is tormented". During the course of the eight chapters we see the boy Arutiun learn the family trades of wool-gathering and carpet-weaving, take up playing the lute as he grows older, appointed as musician to a pleasure-loving prince who suddenly dies, join and later leave a monastery, become very weary in his old age, and finally die. The epilogue has him being led along a path by two angels, who fetch his lute and play it.

The Muse seems to represent the female side of the poet's character. She is the channel through which his grief at the prince's death is expressed, and in his old age she comes as an angel to grant him absolution and death. There is a strong implication of bisexuality, in the sense that there are male and female elements in all of us.

*The Colour of Pomegranates* is clearly not a conventional biography; there is no reference, for example, to Sayat Nova becoming an archbishop. What the director is doing is to use the historical character as a symbol for the sufferings of Armenia over many years, including the 1916 massacre, despite this having occurred generations after Sayat Nova lived; the earthquake of 1988 can be regarded as a chilling further chapter. By implication, these sufferings are associated with those of Christ. The numerous Armenian religious, literary, musical, and artistic references, with their strong nationalistic undertone, possibly explain why the Soviet authorities at the time were so angered by the film.

However obscure the references, marvellous shots remain etched on the memory: the pomegranate juice of the prologue, the astonishing colours of the dyed materials, a scene where hundreds of open books are drying on the church roof as the boy lies in their midst, the way the carefully-posed groups of actors gaze expressionlessly at the camera like religious icons, as we listen to the poetry being narrated (and read the sub-titles, which is inevitably distracting). *The Colour of Pomegranates* is certainly a landmark of post-war Soviet cinema, a film whose obscurities are more than matched by its originality and startling visual imagery.

# COOL HAND LUKE
## Stuart Rosenberg, USA, 1967

*Cool Hand Luke* is in the "prison movie" genre, and on the face of it has nothing to do with religion. It is clearly allegorical, however, with several direct Christian references and an overall theme which seems to identify the central character as a kind of Christ-figure.

Luke, played by Paul Newman, is arrested for breaking the tops off parking meters during a drunken spree. For this relatively trivial offence he is sent to a chain gang, where he remains cool despite extreme pressure. The convict "boss" of the gang, Dragline, takes a strong dislike to Luke and beats him up in a fist fight. Luke, however, wins the respect of the inmates first by fighting back against the cruel guards, then by winning at poker, then by eating fifty hard-boiled eggs for a bet.

Luke's paralysed mother is brought to visit him and to reproach him for leaving her; she later dies, causing him such consternation that he has to be disciplined. Twice he escapes and is recaptured. The camp authorities, anxious to ensure that Luke's independent spirit does not affect the sheep-like attitude of the other inmates, set out to break his spirit by every trick they know.

As a ruse to give himself another chance of escaping, but at the risk of losing face with the other inmates, Luke pleads with the guards to let him be. He and Dragline manage to escape and hide in a church, but the latter goes to fetch the guards. Luke is captured and killed, but dies knowing that his spirit could not be broken.

Purely on the level of a thriller and prison-movie, *Cool Hand Luke* is an excellently-acted and beautifully-photographed film. It also has a certain authenticity, being based on a novel by Donn Pearce (who also co-scripted and acted) drawing on his own experiences in a chain gang camp. It is Luke's dwelling among sinners, his being prepared to suffer for the other convicts who become his "disciples", and for being the "man who will not conform" (to use the film's catch-phrase), which makes him a kind of Christ-figure. His punishment is wildly out of proportion to his crime (clearly the allegory is very loose, because there *was* a crime). After his fist-fight with Dragline there is a shot of him with a white towel over his head, surrounded by "disciples", a clear reference to a popular Biblical image. The eating of the eggs can be seen as a symbolic reference to the source of life. When Luke is hiding in the church, before his death, he talks to God: a Garden of Gethsemane perhaps.

I have no wish to deny the right of viewers to see a film like *Cool Hand Luke* purely as entertainment, or escapism, or a straightforward thriller. I merely point out that the Christian references are very clearly and deliberately there, that they are in no way forced or alien, and that it can make watching such a film a far more interesting experience.

Further, to look below the surface of a commercial movie like this, to see references pointing beyond itself, can lead one to enjoy the more "difficult" film which treats its material in an unconventional and unfamiliar way. A film like Bresson's *Pickpocket*, for example, is on the face of it a crime thriller, but one whose language (filmic as well as actual) creates a barrier for viewers who have only experienced Hollywood-style movies. Only when *Pickpocket* is seen first and foremost as a religious allegory, to which the "thriller" element is fairly incidental, can it be enjoyed and appreciated.

So *Cool Hand Luke* can definitely be classified as a religious film, as well as a "prison-movie". This is just one illustration of how confusing, and even pointless, it can be to classify a film as belonging to one or other of a number of "genres".

# DAY OF WRATH
## Carl Dreyer, Denmark, 1943

Carl Theodor Dreyer must certainly be counted as one of the great spiritual directors of the cinema. After an active career during the silent era he made just four sound films in over 40 years. *Day of Wrath*, the second of these, was based on the Norwegian play *Anne Pedersdotter*, by Wiers Jensen, from which John Masefield derived *The Witch*.

Set in 1623, when witch-burning was rife in the dour religious atmosphere of Denmark, the film can also be seen as an allegory of Denmark under the Nazis; in fact Dreyer spent part of the war in Sweden for his own safety. It has affinities with Ingmar Bergman's *The Seventh Seal*, despite being set in a much later age and having a more straightforward "realistic" plot.

The story centres around a young woman, Anne, unhappily married to an elderly pastor, Absolon, and deeply resented by her mother-in-law. Early in the film Martin, Absolon's son by his now-dead first wife, returns home after a long absence. His homecoming coincides with the trial for witchcraft of an old woman, Marthe. It is Absolon who signed the decree for Marthe's trial, and in whose house she was found hiding. To the sound of singing choirboys the old woman is horrifyingly burned, as Anne and Martin look on.

This dramatic moment brings the two young people close together; they fall in love and spend some idyllic afternoons in the woods. Anne tells Absolon that she has never loved him, while Absolon admits that he was wrong to marry her and starts feeling guilty about Marthe's death. Word spreads that Anne is wishing for her husband's death, and when he does in fact die from a heart attack his mother accuses Anne of witchcraft. She is put on trial and tortured. First Martin, then Anne herself, come to believe that she really is a witch. She resigns herself to her situation and prepares to meet her own death.

On the face of it this rather macabre story is not perhaps one which would appeal to many, but Dreyer's superb style of filming makes *Day of Wrath* thoroughly worth seeing. While lacking the succession of exquisitely long-held shots which make his two later films, *Ordet* and *Gertrud*, such hypnotic masterpieces, the deliberately slow pace and painterly black-and-white images help to transport the viewer into the austere atmosphere of the time and place being evoked. The gentle horizontal and vertical camera movements, and strong sense of rhythm, make this an extremely "formalistic" film, very much classical rather than romantic. As in Dreyer's silent classic *The Passion of Joan of Arc* there is frequent use of the close-up, with the camera lingering on a face or a hand, waiting for a particular look or movement. Dreyer was a superb exponent of the use of lighting to create an almost transcendent atmosphere, and this is much in evidence here. The quietly intense acting also contributes to the overall effect.

The film is primarily, perhaps, about the struggle between good and evil, and about Anne's endurance of this both in society and within herself. Her coming to believe that she may after all be a witch seems bizarre to us today. The 17th century, however, was a time when society took such possibilities for granted, and Anne is a child of her time, just as we are children of *our* time and are influenced, often unconsciously, by societal forces which would seem strange and even evil in another era (the fascination of millions of British people with horoscopes is a good example). This brings us back to the notion that *Day of Wrath* can be seen as a comment on Nazi atrocities, often committed by people so conditioned by their society that they seem not to have recognised the evil of their deeds.

# DIARY OF A COUNTRY PRIEST
Robert Bresson, France, 1950

It is a good rule-of-thumb that great novels make poor films, while bad novels can make great films. This is because films are concerned with the physical actions of the characters whereas novels are more concerned with their internal states; the screen and the page are totally different mediums.

The supreme exception to this rule is the French writer Georges Bernanos' masterpiece *The Diary of a Country Priest*, which became an equally great film at the hands of Robert Bresson. Bresson succeeded because he managed to portray on the screen the very soul of his protagonist.

The novel is in the form of a diary, with daily or less frequent entries written by the young curate of the village of Ambricourt. The film follows this form faithfully; we see entries being written, the narrator reading them out, and the action portrayed simultaneously. (In the version of the film available in Britain the narration, but not the dialogue, is in English.) By this means the film *becomes* a diary, making it more like the abstraction of literature.

The other basic technique used by Bresson is to minimise all expressionism in acting, decor, music, etc. In particular, in all his eleven films from this one onwards (although not in his previous two) nearly all his actors are non-professionals, whom he trained to speak in a fast dull monotone, a technique which professional actors would never have stood for. This unlikely-sounding approach, coupled with the austerity of everything else on-screen, has the effect that the viewer becomes involved not with the external happenings but with the internal state, even the soul, of the characters. They are like icons: totally expressionless but with a real hidden depth if we are prepared to *feel* them with our eyes. This is what makes *Diary of a Country Priest* one of the greatest religious films; it is infinitely more than a mere visual portrayal of a series of events.

The story tells of the young priest's battles against the worldliness of the villagers, his feelings of total inadequacy, and his own ill-health. The main characters with whom he is concerned are the inhabitants of the local chateau: a countess embittered over her son's death, her husband, their unhappy daughter, and the daughter's governess who is also the Count's mistress. In the great central scene of the film the priest succeeds in breaking down the Countess' bitterness and bringing her peace; just in time, because that night she dies (her daughter blames this on him). In his worsening physical state he visits a specialist who diagnoses terminal stomach cancer. Finally he goes to visit a former colleague and dies there, his last words being that "all is grace". This is accompanied by the image of a bare cross which fills the screen, and we know that this priest, who thought he was so inadequate, is in fact a saint.

The effect of seeing *Diary of a Country Priest*, far from being depressing, is wholly exhilerating. Conventionally the hero is not supposed to die at the end of a movie, but to defeat his enemies and live happily ever after. Under Bresson's exquisite direction this "hero" is seen to die and, by implication, to triumph as a result, which is of course a basic Christian tenet. (This is something of an obsession with Bresson, whose protagonists *usually* die at the end of his films.) The final image of the cross is what the film writer Paul Schrader has described as a moment of "stasis", when all that has gone before reaches its culminating point of stillness. Bresson's achievement is to express in a 20th ·century art form something comparable to the achievements of the great religious painters of past ages. It is regrettable that this distinctly uncommercial film is hardly ever shown in this country.

# EUROPA '51
## Roberto Rossellini, Italy, 1952

The character of the "holy fool" is one particularly associated with the literature and cinema of Russia, such as Dostoevsky's *The Idiot* or some of Tarkovsky's films. It recurs in this rarely-shown English-language movie of Rossellini, with Ingrid Bergman as a woman whose sudden adoption of saintliness leads people to think she is mad.

Known also as *No Greater Love*, the film concerns Irene, a shallow, pleasure-loving, rich young woman who undergoes a total personality change when her only child kills himself because he thinks she has lost interest in him. Seeking a way to use her great inner resources of love she first turns to her Communist cousin Andrea, who urges her to work for the material welfare of others. Irene goes to work in the slums, makes new friends of a very different kind, and does a day's factory work in place of a woman who is in need.

She finds all this unsatisfying, however, and turns to giving help of a less material kind. She cares for a dying prostitute and helps a juvenile delinquent to escape. Her husband, concerned about her sanity, sends her to a psychiatric clinic, where she insists that her actions are morally inspired. This convinces the authorities that she really is mad, and she is incarcerated permanently, even passing up the opportunity to leave.

There is no question that Irene is perfectly sane; none of the tests carried out on her at the clinic reveal anything abnormal. Nevertheless the notion of somebody denying their own comforts on purely moral grounds seems so crazy that both her husband and the psychiatrists assume that she *must* be sick. This attitude is common in Britain today, when "do-gooder" is almost a term of abuse.

The film does not particularly identify with Irene's point of view. It is, in fact, somewhat in the nature of a documentary about the poor and downtrodden of the city, with long-held shots of the slums, and the portrayal of the factory work as utterly degrading. It is also about types of genuinely charitable action which, according to Rossellini, were not unusual in Italy in the very precise period in which *Europa '51* is set, the few years after the Second World War.

This documentary aspect makes it something of a "message picture", which some may not particularly like; it hurries along from scene to scene as if simply pushing home a series of disconnected facts, or opinions, about society. This aspect is redeemed, however, whenever Ingrid Bergman/Irene appears (*can* we separate a famous actress from her rôle?), and we sense her inner spiritual state. This changing inner state is given visual expression by the way her face is lit during the film, ranging from dark at the outset to strikingly bright at the end when she has reached an inner certainty.

Some viewers may be put off by the "social message" aspect. More fundamental, however, is the other "message", the need to love one's neighbour as oneself even if it means being scorned by society, although for the reason given above I am not sure to what extent the director is advocating this. Only a few, like Irene, will achieve this degree of selflessness, for it is almost the hardest thing in the world voluntarily to forgo the pleasures and comforts of life and to risk rejection by family and friends. It may be argued by cynics that Irene is merely seeking self-fulfilment in her own way, and is not really motivated by disinterested love. However, surely the two go hand in hand. For the person who has reached a high degree of spirituality (whatever we mean by that), self-fulfilment *is* found in giving oneself totally in love and sacrifice for others.

# EXTERMINATING ANGEL, THE
## Luis Buñuel, Mexico, 1962

Buñuel's films generally fall into the category of "anti-religious" rather than religious, but his surrealistic and comic broadsides against bourgeois morality should not be shunned. *The Exterminating Angel* is an iconaclastic and (for me) enjoyable attack on the attitudes and poses of the upper classes, with the Church coming in for some direct stick only at the end. In its portrayal of the anarchic brutishness which potentially lies behind the veneer of respectable society it is reminiscent of William Golding's famous allegorical novel *Lord of the Flies*, with the difference that *The Exterminating Angel* is not "realistic", i.e. inexplicable things happen.

A wealthy couple have invited some friends back for supper after a visit to the opera. The servants seem strangely nervous, and we sense that something strange is going on when, without explanation, the guests are seen to enter the house a second time. After the meal all the servants save one have left, but the guests and the remaining servant cannot bring themselves to leave, and they spend the night in the host's salon.

In the morning they are still unable to leave, and are confined to the room as if there is an invisible wall in the way. It is not that they are *physically* prevented from going, but that whenever they approach the "wall" they somehow change their minds, as if under hypnosis. This goes on for days and even weeks, during which time they shed all their façades and are reduced to degradation and squalor. One guest dies and is put in a cupboard; two young lovers kill themselves; a woman has hallucinations and produces demons; a brother and sister steal morphine from a sick guest. Other strange things happen, such as the bear which is seen wandering around the house. As hunger sets in, the trapped people even contemplate cannibalism, until a flock of sheep inexplicably and conveniently arrives (not prevented by the "wall").

The ordeal is ended when a woman suddenly points out that they are all in precisely the same positions as they were when first trapped, and that this is the key to their release. Sure enough they all gratefully stagger out of the room, and in the last scene we see them, restored to their original respectability, giving thanks in church. When the service is over the priests try to leave, only to find that some strange invisible force is preventing them, while outside the church a flock of sheep is seen to be entering. . .

The attack on the façades of bourgeois respectability is self-evident. Other aspects of the film can give rise to much speculation, although it should not be assumed that Buñuel necessarily had a reason in mind for every strange event. The final scene seems to imply that the bourgeoisie are incapable of leaving the Church, not because they are physically prevented but simply because they are sheep-like. While this is obviously an exaggerated portrayal (the bourgeoisie comprise only a small proportion of the Church worldwide, and most churchgoers have very good personal reasons for being such) it is certainly the case that there are some, probably not as many as in the past, whose churchgoing is bound up with the kind of attitudes Buñuel is attacking. *The Exterminating Angel* should not therefore be resented or rejected because of this portrayal.

The film is full of repetitions: the repeat of the arrival at the house, people being introduced to one another several times, the same toast being offered over and over again, the repeating of the initial positions which secures their release. Perhaps this is another aspect of Buñuel's attack on conventions, which by definition are incessantly repeated. A most thought-provoking film.

# FRANCIS, JESTER OF GOD
## Roberto Rossellini, Italy, 1950

This loose "biopic" of St. Francis of Assisi and his friars, by arguably the greatest of Italian directors, is taken from episodes in *The Little Flowers of St. Francis*. The stories and legends centered around various of the characters seem to presuppose some knowledge of the subject. In the nature of the enterprise there is no "plot". The cast is mostly non-professional, in line with the neo-realist tradition of *Rome, Open City*. The monks are played by real Franciscans.

Francis has already founded his order. Returning with his friars from Rome through the rain, he apologises to them when they are driven out of a hut. Brother Juniper gives away his habit to a poor man, returning naked to the monks who are finishing the construction of their chapel. John the Simple, inspired to be like Francis, joins the community, and learns that to beat out the flames which are consuming Francis' habit is to do harm to fire. During a visit by Sister Clare, Juniper arrives naked again, and claims to have been tempted by the Devil the night before. He later feeds a sick brother with a pig's foot, having first told the pig what a great opportunity it was to do good; faced with the angry owner, he offers to give his own foot in compensation. He receives Francis' permission to preach and, in what is almost a "short" within the main film, his humility overcomes the cruelty of the tyrant Nicolaio whose camp he sets fire to. After teaching Brother Leone that perfect joy is to be found in bearing injuries, Francis sends out all the brothers to preach, in whatever direction they face after spinning round and falling to the ground.

These Franciscans seem to epitomise what has become a widespread view among ecologically-minded people, that man should be in complete harmony with

nature. The natural forces of fire and water are
the allies, not the enemies, of man, while Francis'
addressing of the birds, and Juniper's of the pig,
are seen as a perfectly normal way to behave. They
are not idle dreamers, but are always on the move:
building their hut, making things, sweeping the
porch, planting corn, cutting one another's hair.

Their joy is expressed in their games. John
plays on the bells, Juniper swings with the children,
and the brothers balance on each other to pick
fruit. The description of Francis in the film's
title evokes the Old Testament image of David
dancing before the Ark of the Covenant, as well as
the modern musical show *Godspell*.

The friars symbolise an absolute purity and
simplicity, a literal carrying out of Christ's perfectionist commands whose nearest equivalent in
other films is perhaps Buñuel's priest in *Nazarin*.
Thus, in a totally wordless episode, Francis kisses
a leper whom he meets, while Juniper uncomplainingly
bears the blows and the near-decapitation received
at the tyrant Nicolaio's camp.

The brothers very much wear their emotions and
personalities on their sleeves. Francis, who is
presented in no way as the leader (if anything
Juniper is the film's central character), weeps at
moments of special emotion. Juniper permanently has
what some would call a silly grin. The elderly and
simple-minded John has difficulty speaking. In
short, none of them wear the "masks" which we all
don for public consumption because we are terrified
of others knowing that we are weak and insecure. It
is this childlikeness (as distinct from child*ish*-
ness) which gives the friars their particular appeal.

Doubtless not all the events portrayed in the
film are strictly historical. This does not matter.
Provided that *Francis, Jester of God* has conveyed
something of the spirit which inspired St. Francis
and his friars, it has served its purpose.

# GOSPEL ACCORDING TO ST.MATTHEW, THE
## Pier Paolo Pasolini, Italy, 1964

Pasolini's character, notably his outspoken atheism, seems a most unlikely one to have produced what is widely regarded as the greatest film about the life of Christ. This just goes to show that spiritually-inspiring art can come from totally unexpected sources, and that one should not discount or ignore the works of those whom some may consider unsavoury.

The idea for the film came while Pasolini was staying in Assisi and had occasion to read through the Gospels. A great admirer of Jesus as portrayed there, and of Pope John XXIII to whom the film is dedicated, he decided to film Matthew's Gospel (he objected to the "St." in the English title) because he found it "rigorous, demanding and absolute", whereas Mark's Gospel was "too obviously written for people of little education", Luke was "too literary and mellifluous", and John was "too much a mystic to be transmitted visually".

The film keeps almost exactly to the dialogue from the Gospel, while changing the chronology somewhat, omitting several episodes, and including a scene of the dance of Salome which comes from Mark. It is worlds away from the traditional Hollywood approach of great spectacle with famous "stars" hamming it up, being more akin to a mixture of documentary-style neo-realism and the stark austerity of Robert Bresson's films. The actors, nearly all non-professionals, were chosen for their faces rather than their ability, and were told simply to be themselves rather than to act. Jesus is played by a Spanish student, Enrique Irazoqui, who happened to be visiting Rome and who had just the sombre expressionless look which Pasolini wanted. (He was dubbed into Italian.) There are splendid performances by Marcello Morante, a lawyer, as Joseph, and by Pasolini's own mother Susanna as the Virgin Mary at the time of the Passion, despite looking about 50 years older than the actress playing the young Mary. There are numerous close-ups of unglamorous peasant faces, reflecting Pasolini's view that true humanity is to be found most of all in such people.

The location shooting was done in Southern Italy, which the director found to be sufficiently similar to Palestine. One of the most memorable sequences, the Sermon on the Mount, was shot in the studio with a dark background and with cuts implying several different scenes; this is in accordance with the general view of Biblical scholars that the Sermon was a collection of sayings from different occasions which were strung together when written down. Particularly impressive use is made of the background music, which ranges from a Congolese Mass to Billie Holiday to Bach's *St. Matthew Passion*.

There is no attempt to go in for "special effects" in the miracle scenes. The healing of a leper is shown simply by a cut from the man's deformed face to his unmade-up one, while the "walking on the water" is obviously "walking on a raft". The lack of spectacle results in the 5,000 who were fed from a few loaves and fishes being reduced to about 50. Some may consider these features to be drawbacks.

Pasolini's declared aim was to create a "purely poetical and natural, non-denominational" version of the Gospel. It is certainly artistic, with tableaux reminiscent of Italian painters like Piero della Francesca and Botticelli. The film does to some extent reflect Pasolini's views, tending to emphasise the aspect of Jesus as a rebel against established society, but there is nothing in it to offend Christians. *The Gospel According to St. Matthew* is an extremely moving film with some highly memorable scenes, and is undoubtedly a landmark in religious cinema.

# KING OF KINGS
## Cecil B. DeMille, USA, 1927

The most famous silent film about the life of Christ is said to have been seen by some 8 billion people worldwide. I find such claims somewhat ludicrous (8 billion is more than the total current population of the earth), but it is certainly an important film, and much better than the 1961 movie of the same name.

It covers the period from the redemption of Mary Magdalene to Christ's Ascension, and tends to improve as it progresses. The early scenes are pure melodrama, with the luxury-loving Mary Magdalene angry because her lover Judas(!) has been lured away by a carpenter. She storms off to see this man, only to find herself falling in love with him.

This fantasy-section fortunately gives way to a more conventional, almost reverential treatment of incidents from the rest of Jesus' life, including the temptations, the raising of Lazarus, the driving out of the money-changers, and the teaching of the Lord's Prayer. Several scenes, such as the calling of the Twelve and the discussion of the payment of taxes to Caesar, were omitted from the final version. The second half of the film concentrates on the Passion, including the trial, Crucifixion, Resurrection, and Ascension.

Jesus is played movingly by H. B. Warner, a silent movie actor who appeared almost 30 years later in a minor rôle in DeMille's last film, *The Ten Commandments*. The ability to convey emotion and other inner states through facial expression is, of course, far more important in silent films than in talkies, and Warner manages this admirably. Particularly powerful is his first appearance, as we see him through the eyes of a blind girl during her healing. The characterisations of the Twelve are distinctly drawn, showing the care which DeMille took to create "real" personages.

Much ballyhoo surrounded the director's attempts to show the utmost reverence for his subject. Two clergymen were present throughout the filming to give advice; one wonders what they made of the ludicrous portrayal of Mary Magdalene's life before her conversion. Warner was allowed to be addressed only by DeMille himself when in costume, was transported in a closed car and wore a black veil when leaving it for the set, was instructed not to be seen in public during production, and had to eat alone in a tent when on location. Shooting did not start until prayers had been said by representatives of various religions, including Islam and Buddhism, and Mass was celebrated every morning on location. Prayers were said at the filming of the Crucifixion. While DeMille was undoubtedly a firm and sincere Christian believer he was also a great showman, and one wonders to what extent these elaborate preparations were motivated by the desire for publicity.

Along with the ballyhoo went much controversy. The fact that Caiaphas rather than Judas was made responsible for Christ's death did not prevent vociferous Jewish criticisms. Among other things DeMille was accused of having a warped sense of religion, of being a propagandist for Christianity, and of having bad taste.

Fashions in the cinematic portrayal of Christ invariably change, and Warner's performance, as well as the film's style generally, would seem quaint to many in present-day audiences. This *is*, however, just a matter of fashion rather than of any innate superiority (other than technical, such as sound) of more modern versions. No portrayal can hope to capture "what really happened", and if it were possible to be transported back to first century Palestine we would probably be astonished at how people actually spoke and behaved. *King of Kings* remains an interesting landmark in the history of these ever-changing fashions.

# LANCELOT DU LAC
## Robert Bresson, France, 1974

I found *Lancelot du Lac* infinitely more impressive and enjoyable in the cinema than on television, and can only put this down to the fact that, as with most of Bresson's films, it requires uninterrupted concentration to which the medium of television is simply not suited. His austere and elliptical style, where so much has to be actively inferred by the viewer, seems to require the big screen and the darkened auditorium.

Like most films set in the Europe of centuries ago it portrays a society where religion is taken for granted as being the mainspring of everybody's life. The film, which Bresson had been planning to make for 20 years, is a version of the Lancelot and Guinevere legend. Lancelot, returning with the surviving Knights of the Round Table from a fruitless quest for the Holy Grail which he wishes to continue, tells Guinevere that he has vowed to God not to become her lover. Guinevere reminds him that he is bound by a previous contrary vow to her. King Arthur suggests to Lancelot that, by keeping himself from Guinevere in defiance of his vow to her, he is provoking God's wrath. This prompts the knight to urge Guinevere to release him, which she does.

There follows a jousting scene in which Lancelot proves his abilities to all. He is wounded, however, and rides off to the forest to be cared for by a peasant women who foretells his death. On returning he agrees to restore Guinevere to the King, joins Arthur in battle against a rebellion, and is killed along with many others by a new weapon, the bow and arrow.

*Lancelot du Lac* is a highly stylised, "un-realistic" film. The opening shot is of knights, totally clad in armour, toppling over with fountains of blood spurting out of them, while the closing shot is of an enormous heap of suits of armour after the battle, like so much scrap metal. For most of the remainder of the film men are clanking around in suits of armour, leading some otherwise intelligent critics at the time of the film's release to denounce it as boring and pointless. One hopes that they have changed their minds by now.

The high point of the film is the jousting sequence. Shot at about knee-height, we see Lancelot repeatedly mount, charge, dispatch an opponent, and return; more precisely, we do not *see* him as he is encased in armour, but we know it is he because his name is spoken each time by the watching Gawain. This beautiful, poetic, rhythmic sequence is like an Uccello painting in motion, and it is no surprise to learn that Bresson wanted to be a painter in his younger days.

One notable feature of this film, indeed of many of Bresson's films, is the frequent shots of birds and animals. In *Lancelot du Lac* there are enormous close-ups of the eyes of frightened horses, magpies which appear outside the window when Lancelot and Guinevere are talking of their love, crows perched on skeletons and pennants. It is as if the animal world is more perceptive than the humans and is commenting on man's weaknesses.

As mentioned above, some critics could not see what Bresson is getting at in *Lancelot du Lac*. I think it is a lament for a "golden age". He is regretting the passing of an era when men's lives were governed by a code of honour based on religious certainty, when for example Gawain, while also in love with Guinevere, could not be other than totally loyal to both Lancelot and Arthur. That "golden age" was ended by the invention of the crossbow, and Bresson is implying that technological advance generally makes the world a worse place. If this interpretation is correct, it is in keeping with the bleak, pessimistic outlook of his subsequent films, *The Devil Probably* and *L'Argent*.

# LEGEND OF THE HOLY DRINKER, THE
Ermanno Olmi, Italy, 1988

Without ever being regarded as among the top rank of directors, Ermanno Olmi has made consistently interesting films over the years, from the point of view of a kind of social Catholicism. *The Legend of the Holy Drinker* must be virtually the most international film ever made, with an Italian director, a Parisian setting, a Dutch star, English-language dialogue, and a German short novel (or long story) as its source.

Andreas (Rutger Hauer) is a Polish ex-miner now living as an alcoholic underneath a bridge of the Seine. An elderly gentleman (Anthony Quayle) approaches Andreas and offers him a loan of 200 francs, suggesting that he repay it to the priest at a particular church which contains a statue of St. Thérèse of Lisieux, to whom the gentleman is indebted for an unspecified miracle.

The feckless Andreas is hardly the type to keep money for long, and most of the film consists of his getting rid of the money in various ways, only to find that it keeps reappearing. After spending the gentleman's note on an expensive meal and plenty to drink, he is offered 200 francs to help a man with his house removals. Dutifully going to the church but finding that it is the middle of Mass, he waits in a café only to meet his ex-lover, whom he takes for another expensive meal. He buys a second-hand wallet and discovers 1,000 francs in it. Further attempts to repay the debt are thwarted by more binges and encounters with old acquaintances: a boxer, a dancer, a colleague from the mines.

Back at the Seine Andreas again meets the elderly gentleman, who claims not to recall their earlier meeting but nevertheless lends him another 200 francs. This goes in payment of a bar bill, but while waiting in the café opposite the church a policeman gives him a full wallet he has supposedly dropped. Andreas suffers a heart attack, is carried into the church, and dies near the statue of St. Thérèse.

The film's epitaph is: "May God grant us all, all of us drinkers, such a good and easy death." These rather cynical words are imbued by Olmi with a certain spirituality, the implication being that Andreas, a "sinner" in conventional terms (although a thoroughly likeable and genial character), has achieved a kind of redemption. His intentions are honourable and worthy throughout, and his failures are due purely to human weakness.

This spiritual intention of the director is evidenced by his style, with its very slow pacing (the story can be read in about one-third of the time the film lasts) and its almost dreamlike images of Paris, swathed in blue-green light. Andreas also has two visions of a child, calling herself Thérèse, who gently reproaches him for not having visited her.

There are no great theological profundities in this film, which is more a kind of fable than a "realistic" story. The fact that money keeps finding its way back to Andreas can be seen as a series of either miracles or coincidences, according to choice. Director Olmi probably prefers the former, but Joseph Roth's story, with narrative interjections which pour cold water on the idea of miracle, suggests the latter. There is no reason whatsoever why a film should not radically change the emphasis of the book on which it is based, and Olmi is perfectly entitled to do this; as a result, however, the film falls short of being anything approaching a "spiritual" experience, though it is enjoyable and even beautiful. Rutger Hauer's performance is splendid (although he looks remarkably clean for a down-and-out), and a string of mostly French actors, plus the late Sir Anthony Quayle, perform their rôles more than adequately.

# MAN FOR ALL SEASONS, A
## Fred Zinnemann, GB, 1966

This film version of Robert Bolt's play about one of the quintissentially great Englishmen, Sir Thomas More, is one of those well-made, worthy British movies which is certainly worth seeing once but somehow does not draw one back for repeated viewings. Nevertheless it does serve as a reasonably informative presentation of some of the issues involved in one of the most turbulent times in English history.

In 1529 More succeeds Cardinal Wolsey as Lord Chancellor. When Henry VIII wants to divorce his barren wife Catherine of Aragon to marry Anne Boleyn, More makes his beliefs known about the indissolubility of marriage. The Pope refuses Henry's request, and as a result the King declares himself head of the Church in England. When the bishops go along with this, More has no option but to resign.

Thomas Cromwell and others urge the King to demand from More a writ of allegiance to him as head of the Church and State. When More, out of conscience, refuses, he is sent to the Tower of London. Cromwell wants More executed quickly and fabricates charges against him. Found guilty of high treason, More is beheaded, but not before delivering an impassioned speech against his enemies, including the King.

Repeating his stage rôle, Paul Scofield is impressive as Thomas More, conveying dignity, humour, and a quiet determination not to sacrifice his principles even at the cost of his life. Being something of a hagiography the film inevitably does not present a fully-rounded portrait of the man, but Scofield makes the best of this limitation. There are fine performances from the other participants, notably Robert Shaw as a swashbuckling Henry VIII, and Wendy Hiller and Susannah York as More's wife and daughter; the final family parting in the condemned cell is particularly moving.

As just suggested, one of the issues raised by *A Man For All Seasons* is the very nature of film biography. There is a tendency for cinematic portrayals of notably virtuous and admirable historical figures to present them as totally impeccable, and as people whose every move and utterance we are encouraged to think of as perfectly meeting the needs of the situation. This is perhaps a limitation of the cinema; even a lengthy feature film cannot convey a fraction of the "facts" about a person that a written biography can, and inevitably it becomes highly selective and distorting. This is why, in my view, the most interesting films about historical characters are those where the film-maker uses his subject for some wider purpose: for me the two greatest such films are *Andrei Rublev* and *The Colour of Pomegranates*, and it is significant that little is known of the lives of their heroes.

Having said that, there is no doubt that Sir Thomas More, canonised by the Catholic Church in 1935, had admirable qualities to which most people barely begin to aspire. It is perhaps tempting to allow ourselves to think that 16th century England was so barbarous that the imminence of one's own violent death was not nearly as horrifying a prospect as it would be today, and that it was therefore not difficult for More to stick to his principles. This assumption is quite unwarranted. Too often today (and probably at all times) people are persuaded to bend their principles when it suits their convenience, to abandon them if life becomes more congenial by so doing. This happens in both public and private life, and the example of Thomas More is one for all to seek to emulate. This is not to condone fanaticism, but More was certainly no fanatic. *A Man For All Seasons* is a fine illustration of the importance of maintaining one's own integrity.

# MIRROR
## Andrei Tarkovsky, USSR, 1974

It took several viewings before I came to
regard *Mirror* as one of the most perfect works of
art the cinema has produced. While it has little
explicit reference to religion, it is an intensely
soul-searching, poetic, semi-autobiographical mixture
of dreams, memories, and fantasies, set against the
unfolding of modern history. The spirituality is
just below the surface throughout.

With the leading actress and two child actors
each playing two rôles, and unannounced flashbacks
and flashforwards spanning 30-40 years, a first
viewing can be rather confusing. Basically, there is
an unseen narrator, Alexei, a man of about 40 in the
1970s, who recalls his childhood in the late 1930s.
The wonderfully expressive actress Margarita
Terekhova plays Alexei's mother in the 1930s and his
wife in the 1970s. Two child actors play the boy
Alexei at different ages (about 5 and 12) in the
1930s, and his son Ignat at different ages in the
1970s. Once this is grasped, things should be clear.

The director has said that nearly everything
portrayed in the film actually happened in his, or
his mother's, life. For the 1930s scenes he returned
to the remote rural spot where he grew up and built
a replica of the dacha (wooden house) as he
remembered it. The scenes from Alexei's (and
Tarkovsky's) childhood include his first sight of a
building on fire as he stands entranced at the
beauty of the flames, a richly comic sequence in
which his mother fears she has made a dreadful
mistake in her proof-reading job at the State
printing works, and some beautiful memories of his
mother washing her hair and of his father returning
home after a long absence. The 1970s scenes include
Alexei's discussions with his wife, who accuses him
of identifying him with his mother (as stated above,
the actress is the same), and the visit of some

Spanish friends to Alexei's Moscow flat, sparking off the first of several newsreel sequences, this one from the Spanish Civil War.

These newsreel sequences, some of them exceptionally moving, enrich the film greatly, putting the events of Alexei's personal life into a necessary historical perspective. They include the liberation of Prague in 1945, the dropping of the atomic bomb over Hiroshima, and the Sino-Soviet border clashes of the late 1960s. Most moving and beautiful of all are some shots of Soviet troops painfully pulling their armoury across Lake Sivash during the war; we can almost *feel* their physical anguish, while on the soundtrack is spoken a poem about immortality.

This is one of several poems written and spoken by Tarkovsky's own father, generally accompanying the camera's explorations of the dacha and its environs. Here the spirituality becomes more evident, with the poet (and, by implication, the film-maker) in the rôle of one who can conjure a kind of eternity by his use of words or images about a particular moment.

The most explicitly religious reference in the film is a scene where the 12-year-old Ignat, apparently alone in his father's flat, comes across a strange woman (a ghost?) who asks him to read to her from a particular book. This turns out to be a letter written by Pushkin to a 19th century advocate of Russia becoming Roman Catholic. Pushkin argues that Russia's special position meant that she could never be fully part of Europe, with which Catholicism was specially identified, and so should maintain her traditional Russian Orthodoxy. One would guess this was Tarkovsky's own view.

Each subsequent viewing of *Mirror* brings a greater appreciation of its artistic and spiritual integrity. A Westerner cannot expect to understand it as readily as a Russian, but it remains a deeply moving and contemplative experience.

# MISSION, THE
## Roland Joffé, GB, 1986

One of the best commercial films of the 1980s, *The Mission* tells of events which occurred in 1750 which raise interesting and difficult questions about the Christian response to aggression by secular interests.

The Papal legate Altamirano is writing to the Pope about his visit to the mission fields of South America. From this opening comes the flashback which lasts almost the entire film, as we see how the idealistic Jesuit, Father Gabriel, goes out to replace another priest who has been killed by the Indians. Gabriel manages to win over the tribe and decides to build a mission station.

Meanwhile the slave-trader Rodrigo Mendoza, having killed his own brother over a woman, suffers deep remorse and is visited by Gabriel. In penance for his crime he voluntarily hauls a heavy load of armour and weapons, relics of his past life, up to the mission, finally being relieved of it by an Indian who sends it crashing down the sheer rock-face which Rodrigo has just scaled. Following this symbolic act of forgiveness for his past treatment of the Indians, he helps with the building of the church and decides to become a Jesuit under Gabriel's authority.

Altamirano arrives to adjudicate between the interests of the Jesuits and those of the European traders who wish to keep the Indians in slavery. When Rodrigo publicly accuses the traders' representative of lying, his vow of obedience obliges him to apologise although we are left in no doubt that his accusation is justified. Altamirano is very impressed by the mission but, fearful of damaging the Church's interests in Europe, he reluctantly sides with the traders' demands that the Indians must leave. When the Indians decide to fight, Rodrigo feels he must take up arms on their behalf, although as this violates Gabriel's authority he has to leave the order. In the inevitable battle both Rodrigo and Gabriel, the fighter and the pacifist, are killed, and the mission is burned down.

*The Mission* is a splendidly-made and enjoyable film. Jeremy Irons and Robert De Niro play Gabriel and Rodrigo, but even the great De Niro is upstaged by Ray McAnally's Altamirano, wonderfully conveying a mixture of cynicism and anguish. Much is added by Chris Menges' stunning location photography and Ennio Morricone's haunting score. The film, scripted by Robert Bolt, is unequivocally on the side of the Indians and the mission, while leaving the viewer to judge which of the two doomed Jesuits has taken the right line. The strong implication is that it hardly matters, as their position is hopeless anyway.

The age-old conflict illustrated in *The Mission*, that between a stand for perfection and principle and a willingness on occasion to make limited compromises with the world, will probably always be with us. In the film it takes two forms: the conflict within the legate himself, and that between the perfectionist Gabriel and the passionate Rodrigo. Viewers will not need the prompting of the film to agree that Altamirano's decision is unequivocally wrong. They will be less inclined to condemn Rodrigo for *his* betrayal of principle, as the notion of obedience to a religious superior is one which these days strikes most people as rather quaint.

Viewers will also have no sympathy for the position of the Church in Europe, as portrayed in the film. To shore up one's institutional position, at the expense of supporting powers of evil in the form of slave-traders, may stave off short-term inconvenience but it cannot be right. To judge with hindsight, and from a different era, is easy, but events such as those portrayed in *The Mission* will always be reminders of the dangers of compromise with the world.

## MOTHER JOAN OF THE ANGELS
### Jerzy Kawalerowicz, Poland, 1960

There are numerous films about strange goings-
on in convents, many of them over-sensationalised
and of no serious interest or merit. One of the
best is this acclaimed Polish offering, based on a
novel inspired by the well-known case of the 17th
century French convent at Loudun. It has something
to say about oppression of any kind, and is
particularly beautifully shot.

Mother Joan is the head of a Polish convent in
the 17th century. She and all the other nuns,
except Sister Margaret, are rumoured to have become
possessed by devils, which were supposedly set loose
by a priest who has been burnt at the stake for so
doing. After four other priests have vainly tried
exorcism, the bishop asks the ascetic young Father
Joseph to see what he can do. Much private prayer
and self-flagellation fail to bring about any change,
nor does it help when he tries to subdue what he
sees as Mother Joan's spiritual arrogance. To
complicate matters he finds himself becoming physically attracted to her; far from being the raving
fanatic of his imagination she is a beautiful and
dignified woman who engages in serious philosophical
discussions. His shy, tender affection seems to be
returned.

Father Joseph seeks the advice of an old rabbi
who suggests that the problem is simply human
nature: Mother Joan is suffering from the absence of
angels rather than the presence of devils. Father
Joseph realises that the rabbi, who is played by the
same actor, is a kind of stand-in for himself. The
priest, increasingly obsessed with the nun, is in a
tragic conflict with himself, his feelings, and his
principles, even putting up a trellis in the attic so
that she cannot come too near. Eventually, in an
extraordinary act of sacrifice, he asks the demons
to leave Joan and enter himself, as a result of

46

which he kills two innocent stable grooms in a tavern. He asks Sister Margaret to tell Mother Joan of his sacrifice on her behalf.

The cast perform with the utmost authenticity, evoking an emotional response in viewers (except those for whom this very serious subject seems to evoke sniggers), while the beautiful photography and austere sets make the film a visual delight. The two main characters have no physical contact, but there is an erotic charge through huge close-ups of faces, eyes, and hands. As for the content, while it may be unappealing it does make legitimate points about oppression, not just religious but by implication political. The film's country of origin is of relevance here. The director has said: "My film is a protestation against the fetters imposed on man from outside, whether Catholic or not." It must also be emphasised, as I point out elsewhere, that to judge the behaviour of one age in history from the viewpoint of another is not very helpful.

How are we to interpret the demons? Many Christians accept the objective reality of such spirits, but it is equally true that, particularly in ages past, people can ascribe demonic forces to phenomena which can be more readily explained in other ways. In the film (which *is* a fiction, not intended to be a representation of the events at Loudon) one could say that the "demons" are the expression of Mother Joan's rebellion against her existence, and of her need for love and spiritual contact. This infects the other nuns, and causes the downfall of the man who, in other circumstances, she might have loved.

In the last resort, *Mother Joan of the Angels* is *not* anti-religion or anti-Church. It is a portrayal of a human tragedy which, in this case, happens to take place among nuns and priests. It is about the rebellion of people seeking their freedom and individuality, which can happen in any environment.

47

# NAZARIN
## Luis Buñuel, Mexico, 1958

One of three Buñuel films included in this book, *Nazarin* is the only example of his work which can be interpreted as being favourably disposed towards Christianity. It must be said, however, that a negative interpretation is equally possible, and in the light of his subsequent films it is clear that the claims that *Nazarin* was the sign of an imminent conversion were premature. The film's ambiguity is ironically illustrated by the fact that it won a prize not just at the Cannes Film Festival but also from the International Catholic Cinema Office.

In the early years of the century, Don Nazario is a humble and unworldly Mexican priest who tries to live out the gospel literally, but who finds that every well-intentioned act invariably leads to trouble. He is ridiculed in his village, and, sheltering a prostitute wanted by the police for murder, succeeds only in arousing the anger of his superiors. He decides to go on the road in order to serve the poor, and is accompanied by the prostitute and a woman he has saved from suicide. Returning to his village he is disturbed to find himself now regarded as a saint and miracle-worker. Arrested as an accomplice to murder, he is imprisoned in a chain-gang and severely beaten up. On the road he accepts the gift of a pineapple from an old woman.

The interpretation by some of *Nazarin* as a Christian film springs from the extremely sympathetic portrayal of the central character, who is invested with great dignity; it is easy to see that Buñuel might be advocating the literal following of the gospel in every respect. Against this interpretation, he is showing the disasters which can result from this course, while the final scene where the priest accepts the gift of a pineapple shows that he is ultimately dependent on material things. I think that *Nazarin* was certainly never intended to be a Christian film, but that the director has admiration for the man who strictly adheres to worthy principles.

*Nazarin* is an exceedingly grim film, the dirty peeling walls of the priest's house symbolising the aesthetic bareness of the film as a whole. It is certainly of no interest to those who want entertainment or spectacle, but raises interesting questions about the Christian life.

To what extent should Christians (and, by implication, adherents of other religions) follow to the letter the moral precepts of their religion? The answer which both Christians and non-Christians would immediately give is "to the utmost". A moment's reflection will show, however, that the positive precepts of a religion's moral teaching (as distinct from the prohibitions) are a limitless challenge; however much one does by way of "good works" it is always possible to do more, so that total adherence is impossible. In a sense, therefore, it comes down to practicalities, in which one should have regard to one's situation in life (material, family, health) in determining one's charitable activities. The Catholic and Orthodox traditions of Christianity have a particular channel, monasticism, for those who wish to strive to go the whole way, and this is what Don Nazario has chosen in Buñuel's film. This does not of course preclude lay people from choosing a similar path if their circumstances permit.

Is Buñuel right in suggesting that striving to go the whole way is self-defeating, by leading only to trouble and disaster? The fact that this happens in *Nazarin* is, of course, simply a reflection of the director's desire to show this. The answer is surely that a person needs the wisdom to discern what is the best course of action in a particular situation. One could say that Don Nazario, as portrayed in the film, lacks in wisdom what he possesses in charity and zeal.

49

# NIGHT OF THE HUNTER, THE
## Charles Laughton, USA, 1955

Critically acclaimed as one of the greatest of American movies, Charles Laughton's only film as a director is a beautifully shot and constructed fable about good and evil, in the form of a thriller, with an astonishing central performance by Robert Mitchum as a self-appointed preacher.

Harry Powell (Mitchum) is sent to prison for stealing a car. His cellmate is a convicted murderer and bank robber who, Powell discovers, has hidden 10,000 dollars at his home and has sworn his two children to secrecy about it. He is soon hanged.

On his release Powell goes to stay in his cellmate's home town, and manages to ingratiate himself with the widow, demonstrating the struggle between good and evil by means of the words "love" and "hate" tattooed on his fingers. The gullible woman agrees to marry this "preacher", only to meet her death at his hands and to end up in the river.

Powell spreads the story that the widow has run off with another man, and tries to befriend the children. When the little girl refuses to tell him the whereabouts of the money he is enraged. The children escape his clutches, find a small boat, and float along through the night, the girl clutching her doll which, we know, contains the money.

In the morning they are awakened by Rachel (Lillian Gish), a middle-aged Christian woman who devotes herself to looking after stray children. After they have lived in her house for some time Powell discovers their whereabouts, and unsuccessfully tries to impress Rachel with his preacher act. Eventually Rachel is forced to wound Powell with a shotgun to protect the children. As Powell is being taken away by the police the boy grabs his sister's doll and smashes it over Powell's head, thus revealing the secret.

A film's director, in my view, is usually the person to whom its artistic success can be primarily attributed. The greatness of *The Night of the Hunter*, however, can be attributed not just to the obviously talented Laughton, but to Mitchum's devastating portrayal of evil, Gish's inevitably wonderful performance, Shelley Winters' impressive portrayal of the widow, the script by the renowned film critic James Agee, and the luminous cinematography of Stanley Cortez: there are marvellous shots of wildlife watching the children float down the river by night, and of the widow floating in the river, her long hair slowly waving in the water. The film is a remarkable mixture of the American silent movie tradition (the "iris-out" and Lillian Gish are both associated with D.W.Griffith), the style known as German expressionism with its stark shadows, and American "primitive" painting. It has also been described as perhaps the most remarkable portrait of childhood in all cinema.

The unusual mixture of evil and horror on the one hand, and a highly poetic style on the other, make the film particularly memorable. The preacher's theme-song is a perversion of an old hymn: "Leaning, leaning, safe and secure from all alarms. Leaning, leaning, leaning on the everlasting arms!" In one unforgettable shot Powell, singing this song, is slowly riding by night along a distant ridge, silhouetted against the sky. Such was Laughton's inventiveness that this was in fact a midget on a pony, in a studio set.

The film can be seen partly as a Biblical allegory, with the widow as Eve, the preacher as the serpent, and the children as the baby Moses. Rachel can perhaps be seen as a Christ-figure, engaged in a cosmic battle with the phony preacher. *The Night of the Hunter* is a marvellous but nightmarish fairy-story, culminating with the triumph of good over evil as all fairy-stories should.

# NOSTALGHIA
## Andrei Tarkovsky, Italy, 1984

*Nostalghia* (the "h" is in the film's title) is the first film Tarkovsky made outside the Soviet Union. It contains much in the way of religious imagery and attitudes, and is a film of exceptional beauty.

The title has far more meaning than the fashionable one of looking back to a pleasant time in the past; it refers to the pain of being away from one's homeland, and the film is certainly semi-autobiographical. As such it can be seen as a sequel to the almost entirely autobiographical *Mirror*, made a decade earlier.

*Nostalghia* tells of a Russian musicologist, Gorchakov, who is visiting Italy to do research on an 18th century composer. As interpreter he has the beautiful Eugenia, a modern, confident woman who is a sharp contrast to the dreamy Gorchakov. When he asks her to visit a chapel with him she wanders around like a tourist, while all the other women there have come to pray.

In the village where Gorchakov is staying he becomes obsessed with a strange recluse called Domenico, a sort of "holy fool" character who thinks everybody else is mad (the feeling is mutual), who has the slogan "1+1=1" painted on the wall of his living-room, and who tells Gorchakov that to save the world he must carry a lighted candle across the local thermal baths without it going out; he has tried to do so himself but has been prevented by the bathers.

Back in the hotel Eugenia has a passionate outburst at Gorchakov, railing at his obsession with churches and mad prophets, and implying that he ought to be interested in more carnal matters, to whit, herself. Gorchakov, who has a wife and children in Russia, declines the opportunity.

Domenico addresses an apathetic-looking open-air crowd in Rome on the dangers of nuclear catastrophe; he then douses himself with petrol and sets himself alight, dying astride a statue as the silent onlookers watch without expression. Meanwhile Gorchakov lights a candle and attempts to cross the now-drained baths. In a single nine-minute shot we see him twice get halfway across before the flame goes out; he succeeds at the third attempt and then collapses. This shot, either stunning or utterly boring according to taste, is an example of Tarkovsky forcing the viewer to have the patience to experience time along with the character.

*Nostalghia* is a "difficult" film; the narrative is clear enough, but what is it meant to be about? To a large extent, homesickness. There are several beautiful dream or fantasy sequences, shot in sepia rather than full colour, showing images of Russia and of Gorchakov's family. The most memorable is the final shot of the film, in which a traditional Russian wooden house, or dacha, is shown enclosed by a vast Italian cathedral, implying that the exile (Gorchakov, Tarkovsky), while nominally "free", is effectively imprisoned.

Another key theme, and of particular interest from a religious point of view, is the character of Domenico. Tarkovsky clearly admires the man who is prepared to sacrifice himself for what he sees as a greater cause; most of his films contain a character of this kind, not least Alexander in *The Sacrifice*, played by the same actor (Erland Josephson) as is Domenico. The notion of being a "fool for Christ", to use St. Paul's phrase, seems important for Tarkovsky, and it is clear from his book *Sculpting in Time* that he believed that the artist, and by implication everybody, has an absolute duty to remain true to his integrity and his principles. The fact that Domenico is regarded as mad is beside the point, as far as this great visionary director is concerned.

53

# NUN'S STORY, THE
## Fred Zinnemann, USA, 1958

A film which is worthy rather than outstanding, tasteful rather than challenging, *The Nun's Story* is based on the novel by Kathryn Hulme inspired by a real-life character, and can be taken as a fairly "realistic" presentation of some of the problems which may face a woman who joins a religious order.

Set in the 1930s, the film tells of Gabrielle Van Der Mal, daughter of a Belgian surgeon, who wants to be a nursing nun in the Belgian Congo (now Zaire). She enters a convent and, in a documentary-like section, her progress from novitiate to nun is meticulously and fascinatingly shown. We see the prescribed prayers and devotions, the kissing of the older nuns' feet, the begging for soup, the hard manual work, the various penances and deprivations. Mother Emmanuel, the Superior General, while admitting that a nun's life is in some ways unnatural, claims that there are earthly as well as heavenly rewards to be gained by adhering to the strict rules of the Order.

Sister Luke, as Gabrielle has now become, goes off to learn tropical medicine, but is then sent to a Belgian mental hospital. Despite being asked to stay away from a particular patient, her pride persuades her that she can handle the situation and she is nearly killed as a result.

When she eventually reaches the Congo she is assigned to a hospital not for Africans but for Europeans, which is something of a disappointment for her. She secretely falls in love with the surgeon Dr. Fortunati, but he is totally wrapped up in his work and has no interest in either women or religion. Deciding to throw herself fully into the task assigned to her she contracts tuberculosis, but is soon cured. Dr. Fortunati attributes her illness to fear of being sent back to the convent in Belgium, although her own motive is a belief that she can only achieve oneness with God by staying in the Congo.

On the outbreak of the Second World War she is asked to accompany a Belgian official back home. Unable now to leave Europe she goes to work in a convent hospital near the Dutch border, and is told to turn the other cheek to the parachuting Nazi invaders. This becomes increasingly difficult, as refugees pour in and she feels her vocational humility increasingly under threat. When, in helping refugees to escape, her father is killed by the Nazis, this proves the final straw; Sister Luke joins the Resistance realising that this will be incompatible with remaining in the Order. She goes through the necessary formalities and leaves the convent to become Gabrielle again.

The film has fine performances from Audrey Hepburn as Gabrielle/Sister Luke, Edith Evans as Mother Emmanuel, and Peter Finch as Dr. Fortunati. Audrey Hepburn could bring a certain authenticity to her rôle, having been born in Belgium of a Dutch mother, having spent the war in Holland involved in the Resistance, and even having had a brother in a concentration camp as does Gabrielle.

Zinnemann is a director of integrity; he has been holding out against the threatened "colorising" of the video-cassette version of his famous Western *High Noon*. In *The Nun's Story* he refused to bow to studio pressure for the usual convention of having music played as the film ends. As a result Gabrielle's final exit from the convent is in complete silence; this is more effective than an emotion-inducing musical theme would be.

The film is unobtrusively shot, and there is a particularly fine sequence in which several dozen nuns are simultaneously going about their tasks (the kind of sequence which cannot come across properly on the small screen). Despite its "tastefulness", *The Nun's Story* is one of the best religious films to come out of Hollywood.

## ORDET
## Carl Dreyer, Denmark, 1954

It is easy for us in secular Western Europe to forget that for most of the world's population, and for the overwhelming majority of people who have ever lived, religion is the primary motivating force of their lives. Dreyer's masterpiece *Ordet*, based on a play by Kaj Munk who was murdered by the Nazis, is set in a turn-of-the-century rural Jutland community where the importance of religion is taken for granted. It is undoubtedly one of the most moving religious films ever made.

The old farmer Bergen lives with his three sons, each of whom presents a problem for him. The oldest, Mikkel, has become an atheist; he has two young daughters and his wife Inger is expecting another baby. The middle one, Johannes, has undergone intense theological study as a result of which he believes that he is Jesus Christ. He is given to wandering from room to room, or up to the heath at night, uttering Christ's words from the Gospels in a slow, piping voice, and is regarded by everybody else (except for one of the little girls) as completely mad. The youngest son, Anders, wishes to marry a girl whose father belongs to a rival Christian sect, a humourless group who consider that they are the only ones who have the truth.

As the film develops in its slow, measured way, Inger goes into labour and it becomes clear that she is having a very difficult time. In a series of emotionally intense scenes the baby is stillborn and Inger herself dies soon after. On the day of the funeral Johannes returns after mysteriously disappearing for a time. The family are shocked when he suggests praying for Inger's return to life but, when his little niece shows that at least *she* has faith in him, he prays for her mother who, Lazurus-like, is immediately resurrected. Her husband Mikkel has his faith restored, while Anders gets his girl when the two fathers patch up their quarrel.

This "happy-ever-after" ending may sound trite and contrived, but Dreyer's intentions are clearly of the highest artistic seriousness. He never cuts unless strictly necessary, and there are marvellous long-held shots, some lasting several minutes, in which the camera, representing the viewer, moves slowly around to capture the action, making full use of the "three-dimensionality" of the set; an actor is liable to exit left and then reappear right, having walked behind the camera (or the camera having moved across in front of him). This contemplative style not only demands a far higher standard of acting than does the familiar frequent-cutting style, but it also provides a sense of authenticity which the film would otherwise lack.

Another notable feature is the lighting effects; this black-and-white film seems to contain innumerable shades of grey to express the changing spiritual state of the various characters. Dreyer himself wrote that the artist must "abstract himself from reality in order to strengthen the spiritual content of his work", and certainly the appearance of *Ordet* is far from being purely representational. The resurrection scene in particular, with the bright sunlight streaming through the windows, is immensely powerful, especially as the first indication of the "miracle" is seen in the child's smile as she confidently holds the hand of her uncle Johannes.

Non-religious people may feel that this resurrection scene is a "cheat". It must be said, however, that "natural" explanations are perfectly possible; people are occasionally wrongly diagnosed as dead. Dreyer leaves us to interpret it as we wish. But Dreyer is fairly evidently on the side of the importance of religious faith (his background was Calvinist). *Ordet* is probably the most intensely religious film set in recognisably modern times.

# OUR TOWN
## Sam Wood, USA, 1940

A delightful and amusing fantasy based closely
on Thornton Wilder's Pulitzer Prize-winning play of
1938, *Our Town* is of particular interest because of
a sequence near the end when a woman is taken into
the world of the dead. The film's main theme is
that happiness is so fleeting that it should be
experienced more intensely while it lasts.

Set in small-town America between 1901 and
1913, it is narrated by Mr. Morgan, a talkative
homespun philosopher who acquaints us with the
characters living in Grovers Corner, New Hampshire,
where he owns the drug store. The film is centered
around two families, the Gibbses and the Webbs, and
the marriage bond which comes to unite them.

Emily Webb (played by Martha Scott) is the
local newspaper editor's daughter, while George Gibbs
(William Holden) is the doctor's son who falls in
love with her. Their adolescent and courtship days
are lovingly portrayed, surrounded by the adult
world which looks on amusedly and delightedly,
especially when they eventually marry.

In the film's last section Emily, expecting her
second child, is lying dangerously ill and foresees
her death. Given the opportunity to revisit a time
in her past life she chooses her sixteenth birthday,
a summer's day when she went on a family picnic to
which George came too. As she sees the others
bustling about, even walking *through* this person who
is visiting from the future, she says to her
unheeding mother: "Just look at me one minute as
though you really saw me!"

From the town cemetary on a hill, the dead of
Grover's Corner look down on the living, as Mr.
Morgan observes that they are "waiting for something
they all feel is coming, something important and
great. Aren't they waiting for the eternal part in
them to come out clear?" He remarks that they don't

stay interested in the living for very long, as the earth part of them burns away and they get indifferent to what's going on in Grover's Corner.

When Emily joins them she is immediately made welcome, and accepts it as perfectly natural that she has now passed from the living to the dead. When George grieves at her grave one of the dead women says: "Goodness, that ain't no way to behave!" to which Emily replies: "They don't understand, do they?"

Obviously this is not intended to be a considered view of what actually happens when we die. The film is a fantasy, with a deeply tender regard for the characters in their joy and their pain, humanism in the best sense of the word. It is moving, compassionate, and funny, a microcosm of smalltown America before the Great War. It is also extremely well made, and has a stirring score by Aaron Copland.

Three great films are brought to mind by *Our Town*. One is Frank Capra's *It's a Wonderful Life* (notoriously "colorised" for video release, a process akin to painting a moustache on the *Mona Lisa*). This is also a portrait of smalltown America, in which the suicidal James Stewart character learns from a visiting angel how worthwhile his life has been. Another is Ingmar Bergman's *Wild Strawberries* (q.v.), one of whose key scenes is where the central character, an old man, revisits in daydream a scene from his youth where the people he is watching are unaware of his presence among them; this film is not a fantasy but makes some similar points to *Our Town*. The third film is Edgar Reitz' 940-minute *Heimat*, shown twice on British television as well as in the cinema, which portrays the life of a German village over 60 years. Not only does it show a great love for its characters in their joys and heartaches, it also ends with the narrator dying and finding himself in a sort of "heaven" with all the people he used to know.

# PASSION OF JOAN OF ARC, THE
## Carl Dreyer, France, 1928

Dreyer's silent masterpiece is regarded as one of the greatest films of all time, with Renée Falconetti's Joan as perhaps the definitive screen performance, never bettered. Of the many films about the Maid of Orléans, only Bresson's *The Trial of Joan of Arc* (q.v.) approaches Dreyer's for sheer spiritual and emotional power.

Offered the chance to make a film about a great Frenchwoman, following the success in France of one of his earlier films, Dreyer chose Joan because he "wanted to interpret a hymn to the triumph of the soul over life". Dreyer wrote his own screenplay after rejecting one he commissioned from the writer of an admired novel about the saint.

The film is broadly in three sections: the setting up of the tribunal, the trial, and Joan's recantation and execution. At the Palace of Justice Joan is charged with heresy and witchcraft, although her real crime was defeating the occupying English army in battle. The court of ecclesiastics, a tool of the English Earl of Warwick, denounces her for wearing men's clothes and claiming to hear the voices of saints. She denies all wrongdoing and prophesies her eventual victorious release from prison.

Ordered to renounce her visions under threat of torture, Joan faints and is returned to her cell. Awakening sick and very weak, she is promised the Eucharist if she signs the confession, but again denounces her accusers. On being carried to the pyre, however, she confesses and is returned to have her head shaved. Seeing a vision of the Crown of Thorns she recants, and demands to be burned. As the execution takes place the crowd turns against those responsible, but are suppressed by the soldiers. Joan has indeed been victoriously released from prison, a martyr who (we presume) is now in the presence of Christ.

So skilfully is the film made that it involves the viewer totally from start to finish of its 2-hour length. It is most famous for its superb use of huge close-ups: in shot after shot we see the souls of the main protagonists laid bare in their faces, warts and all (Dreyer insisted on no make-up being used). The facial details are accentuated by having brilliant white walls as background; there are no "situation shots", so we never actually see, for example, the courtroom as a whole (the same applies in Bresson's film). This is an interesting example of how Dreyer often "broke the rules" of classical film-making, in ways that can be disorientating to some viewers. The startling low camera angles and masterly use of montage assist in creating an emotionally draining experience, with no spoken words. So powerful was the film considered that it was banned in Britain for some time, an unusual example of censorship; did the authorities consider it anti-English propaganda?

But it is Falconetti, in her only film, who is the real triumph. She was a boulevard comedy actress, but Dreyer saw in her exactly what he was looking for. He said that "behind the make-up, behind the pose and that ravishing modern appearance, there was something. There was a soul behind that facade." Her human weakness and spiritual strength are perfectly combined, adding total conviction to both her confession and her recantation. A common criticism of the actress in the Bresson film is that the human weakness is barely shown, although it must be said that the acting style demanded by Bresson is convincing in a very different way; in addition, that film is primarily a record of the trial while Dreyer's is, as its title proclaims, a portrayal of Joan's passion, identifying her with Christ. In my view both are outstanding, but Dreyer's has achieved the status of greatness.

# PICKPOCKET
## Robert Bresson, France, 1959

*Pickpocket* can be viewed simply as a crime thriller about a young man who becomes a successful thief before finally giving himself up. The film states at the beginning, however, that it is *not* a thriller, and indeed on this level it is of little interest except as a documentary about the art of picking pockets. It is far better seen as one of Bresson's fascinating allegories about sin and redemption, perhaps a cinematic equivalent of a Graham Greene novel.

The young intellectually-minded Michel has taken to a life of thieving, and when he is caught robbing a woman at a racetrack he tells the police inspector that to seek danger and self-destruction is the most worthwhile path in life. After his release he reflects on the morality of this, especially when his mother dies a year after he stole money from *her*. His friend Jacques tries to guide him towards the straight and narrow in the form of middle-class respectability, but this does not meet Michel's needs.

When Michel meets a master pickpocket he eagerly learns the tricks of the trade, and there are some fascinating scenes at the railway station and on the Metro which could well provoke accusations of teaching viewers how to steal. Back at the race-track, however, Michel is caught, or rather allows himself to be caught, by the police who had set a trap for him after having had their eye on him (the film has clear analogies to Dostoevsky's *Crime and Punishment*). Finally when Jeanne, the girl he now realises he loves, visits him in prison, he tells her: "What a strange road I had to take to find you."

As usual with this director, the first thing that must be commented on is the total austerity of the film's style. The non-professional actor who plays Michel seems to have been deliberately chosen for his expressionless, anonymous facial appearance. The film writer Paul Schrader likens him to a Byzantine icon, whose unsmiling face and staring eyes invite us to look beneath the surface to see, or feel, what is going on underneath; an icon loses its whole purpose if it is at all "naturalistic". Michel is not a *particular* character, he is Everyman, a sinner like the rest of us seeking salvation in his own way. All the dialogue is spoken in a fast, dull monotone, in keeping with Bresson's view that the merest hint of theatricality distracts us from the characters' inner spiritual struggles. This wholly unrealistic style could be easily lampooned, but Bresson has the directoral skill to ensure that it works, provided the viewer is not looking for "conventional" acting (which in any event is highly stylised in its own way).

I said above that Michel *allows* himself to be caught. On a realistic level this would be almost ludicrous, but *Pickpocket* is allegorical, and this self-surrender (penance) is what Michel knows he must do to accept the possibility of grace and salvation. It is only when he is in prison, probably representing purgatory, that grace comes to him in the form of Jeanne.

Some critics have seen Michel as a latent homosexual, who finds picking pockets a useful way of satisfying his desires. This is reading far too much into the film, however; Bresson is known to have no regard for Freudian psychology.

Pickpocket may be compared with Bresson's 1983 film *L'Argent* (not included in this book), which concerns a young man who is swept up in a chain of events which leads him to become an axe-murderer, finally giving himself up like Michel. This much bleaker film is also about sin and redemption, with a far stronger emphasis on predestination than *Pickpocket*. Both films can be strongly recommended, with *Pickpocket* perhaps being more representative of Bresson's work as a whole.

# PRISONER, THE
## Peter Glenville, UK, 1955

When Cardinal Mindzenty of Hungary was imprisoned in 1948 for rebelling against Soviet domination it was not the first time he had suffered such treatment: four years earlier he was treated similarly by the Nazis for refusing to have a mass said in "thanksgiving for the successful liberation of Budapest from the Jews".

Bridget Boland's play *The Prisoner*, produced by Peter Glenville who also directed the film (effectively a filmed play), was astonishingly *not* based on the Mindzenty case, which was not known about at the time. Further, Glenville was inspired during the play's rehearsal to turn the originally-conceived Monsignor into a Cardinal.

Set in an unnamed East European country, the film is a study of the relationship between a Cardinal (Alec Guinness) accused of treason and his brilliant interrogator (Jack Hawkins), a psychologist who was an old friend of the Cardinal but now belongs to the State hierarchy. Because the two worked together against the Nazis the interrogator knows that his prisoner is impervious to physical torture, and that more subtle means are required to extract the false confession that is wanted, which would cause chaos among the ordinary Catholic people. The interrogation goes on for months, until eventually the examiner thinks he has discovered the prisoner's Achilles heel: he became a priest not because of a sincere calling from God but because he wanted to escape his humble beginnings, and that he never loved his low-living mother.

When the examiner convinces the prisoner that his career in the Church is based on a false premise, the latter begins to crack. At a show trial he confesses to treason, which is ·punishable by death, but as a greater punishment he is set free to walk among the countrymen who once venerated him.

Meanwhile the examiner has himself weakened, and he watches the Cardinal walk free as he awaits his own examination.

There are some exterior shots and an irrelevant love story, marring the claustrophobic atmosphere which the subject requires, but the film's crux lies in the interplay between the Guinness and Hawkins characters. Both actors give powerful and moving performances, while Glenville manages to make the film far more than just "talking heads".

*The Prisoner* proved controversial on its release, provoking different responses from different countries. For Ireland it was "pro-communist", for France "anti-communist", and for Italy "anti-Catholic", and the latter two countries refused to enter it for the Cannes and Venice film festivals.

Interesting religious issues are raised by the film and indeed by the Mindzenty case. The conflict between Church and State has frequently arisen during the course of Christian history, and no doubt will continue to do so indefinitely. It goes without saying that no Christian, least of all an appointed public representative like a priest, should be prepared to deny his faith in any way if required to do so. Naturally this is far easier said than done, and none of us can be sure how we would react if put in such a situation. The Cardinal in the film fears nothing that might happen to him, but breaks because of a past and a weakness which he never thought would be brought to the surface. Most of us would have difficulty in being prepared to face physical punishment, and can consider ourselves lucky in being unlikely ever to be put to this particular test.

The issue becomes more controversial when it is a question of the extent to which the Church and its public representatives should positively act to improve society by "interfering in politics". Doubtless this argument will always be with us.

# RELIGIEUSE, LA
## Jacques Rivette, France, 1966

Rivette is one of the group of young French directors who emerged at the end of the 1950s to create the *nouvelle vague* ("new wave"), films characterised by such features as hand-held cameras, filming in the streets, and jump-cuts which appeared to disrupt the flow of time within scenes. *La Religieuse*, an adaptation of a story by the 18th century writer Denis Diderot, is untypical of that movement, except perhaps in its episodic nature. While its subject-matter is certainly uncongenial to many Christians, it does have some important things to say about oppression and the abuse of religious authority.

Set in 18th century France, the film tells of a young girl, Suzanne, who is forced into a convent because her family does not have the money for a dowry to marry her off. She refuses to take her vows and is sent home, where she is forced to submit. When the Mother Superior dies she is replaced by a brutal woman who locks her in her unhygienic cell with minimal sustenance. After unsuccessfully trying to annul her vows via a lawyer Suzanne is transferred to another convent, which turns out to be a complete contrast; total lack of discipline is surely as bad as its opposite. She manages to escape with the help of Dom Morel, a priest who also was forced into his "calling". However, when Morel tries to seduce her she escapes his clutches, finding work as a laundry girl and finishing up in a brothel. Despairing of her wretched situation she throws herself from the window.

Diderot was something of an anti-Christian propagandist, and it is of interest that the book was not published until after the French Revolution despite having been written in 1760. It was based on a practical joke: Diderot wanted to entice a friend to come to Paris from the country, and wrote him a series of letters purporting to come from Suzanne Simonin, a nun who wanted to annul her vows. When his friend decided to visit her, Diderot wrote that she had killed herself. The book takes this same form of a series of letters.

Rivette first adapted the book for the theatre and only subsequently decided to screen it; it is his most theatrical film. He has described Catholicism as "the absolute peak of theatre", and said that the film came out of the experience of working on the stage.

After approving the script the French authorities promptly prevented the film's appearance in 1966 on grounds of anti-clericalism; this was unusual because French censorship has traditionally operated against films deemed politically subversive. Two years later the ban was lifted when the only change was in the title!

Leaving aside the unsavoury subject-matter, *La Religieuse* has been criticised by some for being irrelevant to the world of today. First this is not true, and secondly it would not matter even if it *were* true; a purportedly serious film does not have to have a "message" or to comment on modern life.

That the forcing of a person into religious life is a scandal goes without saying. It does not do the person any good, and it is a denial of their individuality. It is even worse if the institution is anything like the convents portrayed in *La Religieuse*, but it must be emphasised again that Diderot was a militant anti-clericalist who could hardly be expected to paint a flattering picture of the Church. Nor should we judge the activities of another age by the standards of today; there are practices found perfectly acceptable in past ages which we find abhorrent. And are there not aspects of modern life which people today accept as right and proper, but which our descendants will regard, or even which our ancestors regarded, as totally scandalous?

# ROME, OPEN CITY
## Roberto Rossellini, Italy, 1945

Along with such directors as Bresson, Dreyer, and Tarkovsky, Roberto Rossellini was one of the great conveyors of *spiritual* values in the cinema, although apparently himself an unbeliever. These spiritual values could take the form of a traditional religious subject, like his life of St. Francis of Assisi; or a subtle portrayal of the effect of a new situation or environment on a character's interior state, like the fascinating *Voyage to Italy*; or an uncompromising celebration of the fight for justice and freedom, like his most famous film, *Rome, Open City*.

This film is seldom shown in Britain, despite having been a worldwide success on its release just after the war. It initiated the movement known as "neo-realism" in the Italian cinema, the other widely-known example being De Sica's *Bicycle Thieves*. With its documentary style, location shooting in the streets in Rome, and use of a largely non-professional cast, it was a startling eye-opener for postwar audiences, and remains strikingly impressive today.

Partly inspired by a true event, the film concerns the efforts of a Catholic priest, Don Pietro, to shelter a Communist activist, Manfredi, during the Nazi occupation of Rome. Also involved is Francesco, a Resistance leader, captured by the Nazis on the morning of his wedding; his fiancée Pina (powerfully played by the famous actress Anna Magnani), who is the central character in the early part of the film, is shot down while in pursuit of the vehicle carrying Francesco away.

Betrayed by Manfredi's girl friend Marina, Don Pietro and Manfredi are captured. Because of their refusal to name names, Manfredi is tortured to death in front of the priest, and Don Pietro himself is executed by firing squad after confiding that "it's

not hard to die, it's hard to live". This bleak
ending is tempered by a note of hope, as the boys
whom Don Pietro had been teaching, and who have
witnessed his execution, march back towards the
city, the great dome of St. Peter's filling the
centre of the screen.

The documentary or newsreel style, with its
grainy black-and-white photography, was forced on
Rossellini as the film studios had been bombed and
film stock was hard to come by. It is, however,
highly effective, giving the impression that the
events were being filmed as they unfolded in
actuality; even some German prisoners-of-war were
drafted in as extras. The film is also an
interesting document for social historians as it
provides a valuable picture of how Rome actually
looked at the end of the war.

The spiritual "message" which Rossellini is
clearly trying to convey is that the forces of the
sacred and the secular, represented by the two main
protagonists, should unite in the face of a common
enemy. This idea is underlined by the brief shots
of the Communist during his torture, in which he
strikingly resembles the traditional images of the
face of Christ on the cross.

Another of the film's themes, one that has
perplexed many minds, is how a highly-cultured
people like the Germans can have come to perpetrate
the most obscene bestialities. Rossellini portrays
this by showing the Nazi commander's office as being
adjacent on one side to a relaxation room where
Beethoven is played and on the other side to the
torture chamber. The acting in these scenes is
rather artificial and mannered, contrasting markedly
with the rest of the film; this may well have been
deliberate, as a means of portraying the inhumanity
of the Nazis.

*Rome, Open City* is both historically important
and extremely impressive, and deserves to be far
more widely known in Britain.

# SACRIFICE, THE
## Andrei Tarkovsky, Sweden, 1986

*The Sacrifice* opened its London run in 1987, just days after the announcement of Tarkovsky's death at the age of 54. This added a particular poignancy to a film one of whose themes is the fear of death, and whose emotional power had allegedly reduced hardened critics to tears at the Cannes Film Festival several months earlier.

The film's action takes place within 24 hours. The middle-aged Alexander is living by the sea with his family and friends, including his 6-year-old son who cannot speak as a result of a throat operation. On the evening of his birthday there occurs the ultimate horror, the outbreak of nuclear war: all power goes dead and low-flying jets are heard overhead. Alone in his room, following a bout of hysteria by his wife, Alexander fervently prays to God that, if only things could be returned to normal, he will sacrifice all his possessions and remain silent. That night he dreams (or *is* it a dream?) that, urged on by his eccentric friend Otto, he sleeps with the maid Maria as the only way to save them all. On waking he discovers that all has indeed returned to normal. Remembering his vow he carries out his side of the bargain with God by luring the others away from the house and then setting fire to it. In a celebrated shot lasting several minutes, the house spectacularly burns to the ground as Alexander is driven away in an ambulance. In the final shot his young son, who remains to carry on where Alexander left off, utters his first words of the film: "In the beginning was the Word. Why is that, Papa?"

A short article cannot possibly do full justice to this magnificent, enigmatic, and immensely rich film. The central theme is the need for faith and spirituality as the only way to save the world. In a sense it does not matter whether God has really

70

answered Alexander's prayer; he is presented as a man prepared to act on faith instead of, like some of the other characters, adopting a fatalistic or hysterical attitude.

The film's style matches its substance: the long-held shots lasting sometimes several minutes, with the camera moving very slowly to left or right, cry out for an attitude of contemplation, of watching, listening, and waiting. The sheer technical brilliance of the co-ordination of movements of actors and camera has seldom been bettered in all cinema. The film would be much the poorer with the frequent cutting technique of modern commercial cinema.

*The Sacrifice* is a visual and aural feast: aural, because as in all his films exceptional attention is paid to the soundtrack (it begins and ends with Bach, and there is much beautiful natural sound). The performances, headed by the fine Swedish actor Erland Josephson, are faultless, while the cinematography by Sven Nykvist is magnificent.

It seems to me that there are at least four possible interpretations of the apparent answering of Alexander's prayer, and that Tarkovsky is inviting us to select the one we wish. There is the Christian interpretation, that God indeed responds to Alexander's plea. There is the psychological one, that Alexander is either mad or that he dreamed the whole thing (it is interesting that the rest of his family make no reference to the averting of the war, suggesting that he may have imagined the night's events). There is the "pagan" one, that it is all something to do with the strange encounter with Maria, who is presented as a kind of "good witch". And there is the rationalistic one, that the war would have been averted anyway. The interpretation we adopt will depend largely on our own pre-existing beliefs. But there is no doubt that Tarkovsky, in his masterful way, is urging us all to exercise faith and to stick to our principles and our integrity.

## SCARLET LETTER, THE
## Victor Sjöström, USA, 1926

Nathaniel Hawthorne's famous novel, set in the highly-charged atmosphere of Puritan Massachusetts in the seventeenth century, was turned into one of Hollywood's best silent movies by the great Swedish director Seastrom, the name under which he was known in America. His third American film starred the wonderful Lillian Gish, a shrewd businesswoman as well as a great actress with a flawless moral reputation, who guaranteed that this potentially scandalous story could be filmed without giving offence. The most we see of the adulterous "love affair" is a discreet kiss, proving that the fashion in modern movies for displaying naked couplings is quite unnecessary to convey the power of romantic love. As is generally the case with films based on novels it is a somewhat truncated version, but this is not intended as a criticism.

Gish plays Hester Prynne, the wife of a doctor who disappeared years earlier. She falls in love with the village clergyman, Arthur Dimmesdale, bearing him a daughter, but persuades him that it would be disastrous to reveal his identity as the father because of the adverse effect on his work. The "scarlet letter" refers to the large A, for adulteress, which Hester is made to have embroidered on her breast. When Dr. Prynne suddenly returns and discovers what has happened, he adopts a false persona in order to find the father. He comes to suspect the clergyman, constantly torments him, and prevents Hester, Arthur, and their daughter Pearl from leaving the village. Tortured by conscience, Arthur finally confesses in public and dies in Hester's arms.

Lillian Gish matures convincingly as the film progresses, projecting Hester's thoughts and feelings with great skill. She is powerfully supported in the rôle of Arthur by Lars Hanson, another Swede,

in his first American film. Sjöström as director
brings to the film an underlying tragic darkness of
which a non-Scandinavian would perhaps have found
impossible; certainly none of the three other
versions have any critical standing. In her
autobiography Gish wrote: "I knew that we must have
a Swedish director. The Swedish people are closer
to what our Pilgrims were than we present-day
Americans. He got the spirit of the story exactly.
I never worked with anybody I liked better than
Seastrom."

Scandinavian directors like Bergman, Dreyer,
and Sjöström certainly do seem to have a particular
talent for filming dramas set in times when
practices like the persecution of witches and the
public humiliation of sinners were generally
accepted in society. In *The Scarlet Letter* Sjöström
masterfully combines a powerful sense of darkness
with a wonderful pastoral element, such as the
images of meadows and streams in the opening scene
of people going to church on Sunday morning.

The elderly men who run this Puritan community
seem motivated not by genuine religious conviction
but by a desire to impose conformity. They are more
interested in the *appearance* of righteousness than
in righteousness itself. Hester's "crime" is just
that, a crime against the community's laws rather
than a sin against God. Leaving aside the whole
question of whether a religious institution should
have secular power, it is surely the duty of all
religious people to ensure, as far as they can, that
any strictures they make about personal behaviour
are genuinely the will of God, and do not have
extraneous motivations such as a wish to make
people conform. "Conformity" is, after all, morally
neutral in itself; one can conform to good or to
evil, and there is little merit in conformity (or,
indeed, rebellion) for its own sake. The type of
society portrayed in *The Scarlet Letter* has little to
commend it.

## SEVEN WOMEN
## John Ford, USA, 1965

Best known for such marvellous movies as *My Darling Clementine*, *The Searchers*, and *Stagecoach*, John Ford made many non-Westerns, including this semi-historical drama set in a Chinese mission station in 1935. It was his final film and, while far from his best, is full of interest and extremely beautiful to watch.

Miss Andrews is the strict, lonely woman who runs the teaching mission. She is helped by three other women and by Charles, husband of one of them, while several villagers and children live there also. The tensions inside the mission are matched by gangs of terrorising bandits in the district outside.

The missionaries, including Charles' pregnant wife Florrie, are awaiting the arrival of a doctor. Dr. Cartwright turns out to be an easy-going, rather loose, cynical young woman with whom Miss Andrews is soon at loggerheads. The arguments are interrupted by further arrivals, led by two more women, from a nearby British mission which has been ransacked by bandits. The doctor further weakens Miss Andrews' authority by bringing a cholera epidemic under control, but cannot persuade her to pay for Florrie to go into hospital as she needs to.

When the soldiers guarding the mission have to leave, thereby exposing it to bandit attacks, Charles drives off to find help and is killed. The mission is attacked just as Florrie goes into labour. Dr. Cartwright delivers the baby and offers herself to the bandit leader, using the opportunity to persuade him to spare the other women and children. Miss Andrews is outraged, but the other women realise that the doctor has sacrificed herself to keep them alive. When all have left save the doctor and the bandit leader, the two drink wine together, the latter unaware that the doctor has poisoned it from her medicine chest and that within moments they will both be dead.

This somewhat melodramatic material is excellently acted, notably by Margaret Leighton conveying the frustrated lesbianism of Miss Andrews, Anne Bancroft as Dr. Cartwright, and Flora Robson as a leader of the nearby mission. That Ford's direction is sure-footed goes without saying. In the earlier scenes he uses the technique of having the colour photography very muted, symbolising the relative quietness of the characters' lives (at least on the surface), whereas the bandits' arrival heralds more garish colours thenceforth.

Many of Ford's films compare, unfavourably, conventionally "moral" characters puffed up with their own self-righteousness with "low" characters who wear their vices on their sleeves. In *Stagecoach* the respectable women of the Ladies' League are presented in a very poor light compared with the alcoholic doctor and the saloon-girl they hound out of town. It is not that Ford *approves* of their activities; rather he is a (non-secular) humanist, who loves his characters in spite of their weaknesses. Similarly, in *Seven Women*, the most sympathetic character is the drinking, smoking, blaspheming Dr. Cartwright, who at least manages to achieve something constructive, and is prepared to make the ultimate sacrifice on behalf of others. The least sympathetic, Miss Andrews, is the one who sits in judgement on her.

Self-righteousness is an unattractive quality, best avoided. In the Christian view *all* are sinners, and a person who condemns another for sinning while hiding his own sins does not convince. This should not, of course, lead to the opposite error of condoning or advocating what is wrong; to lead others astray is as reprehensible as hypocrisy. John Ford's last film raises, in a more subtle way than do some of his earlier ones, some thought-provoking aspects of this subject.

## SEVENTH SEAL, THE
## Ingmar Bergman, Sweden, 1956

Between 1956 and 1963 Ingmar Bergman made six films thought worthy of inclusion in this book, and together they provide a fascinating insight into the director's sincere and anguished progression from half-belief to near-atheism.

The first of these, *The Seventh Seal*, is an undoubted masterpiece. Set in the fourteenth century, and inspired by Bergman's fascination with medieval wood-carvings of Death playing chess with his victims, it tells of the anguished knight Block and his cynical squire Jons (Max von Sydow and Gunnar Björnstrand) who are returning home from the crusades to a plague-ridden Sweden. On being confronted by the black-clad and hooded figure of Death, Block challenges him to a game of chess in order to defer, and perhaps evade, the inevitable, so that he may find some meaning in his life after the disillusioning experience of the Crusades.

As he makes his way across the land to the castle where he left his wife 10 years earlier, Block witnesses the plague victims in their agonies, the self-flagellating penitents, the witches being burned, the priests offering salvation through suffering. He senses that if God were really deserving of worship He would not permit all this suffering. He keeps meeting Death who, in between claiming other victims, reminds him that their game must shortly end. Finally Block manages to find a meaning for his life by securing the escape from Death of the young couple Jof and Mia, together with their baby, before dramatically resigning in his game of chess. The film's title refers to the vision of the End in the Book of Revelation (ch.8 v.1).

Jof and his wife Mia, who seem innocently unaware of the sombre happenings around them, provide some of the delightfully light touches in the film. The juggler Jof is played by the stage actor Nils Poppe and Mia by Bibi Andersson, a star of several of Bergman's greatest films. With their young baby they symbolise the Holy Family, and in a typically exhilerating scene Mia is seen gathering wild strawberries (which provided the title of Bergman's next film). The moment of (black) comedy comes where one character finds that the branch of the tree on which he is sitting is being sawn off by Death himself.

The most famous shot in the film comes almost at the end, when Block and his companions are seen being led by Death in a macabre dance. Apparently this shot was decided upon on the spur of the moment, when Bergman noticed that the natural light and clouds were exactly right for the effect he wanted. Because the actors had all gone home, some of the technicians had to don the medieval costumes to play the parts, and as they appear only in silhouette and long-shot the viewer does not notice.

The film's treatment of faith makes it of particular interest. At one point Block exclaims: "I want knowledge not faith, not suppositions but knowledge. I want God to stretch out His hand towards me, reveal Himself and speak to me." Clearly Block is a modern, not a medieval, man.

One senses that Block and Jons represent the two sides of Bergman's religious feelings at the time: the Lutheran pastor's son who knows that belief makes all the difference in life, and the cynic who feels that God is absent and that we may as well base our lives on that assumption. Although the film's emphasis may tend towards the latter view (certainly the presentation of the medieval Church is condemnatory), Bergman is undoubtedly an artist who takes the claims of religion extremely seriously; not as a mere social phenomenon but as something which challenges us all to make a decision one way or the other. This is what makes *The Seventh Seal* not just a beautiful cinematic masterpiece, but a religious film *par excellence*.

# SILENCE, THE
## Ingmar Bergman, Sweden, 1963

The third film of Bergman's trilogy of the early 1960s, following *Through A Glass Darkly* and *Winter Light*, *The Silence* will undoubtedly leave the casual viewer puzzled, perhaps shocked (one or two brief scenes are what are euphemistically called "adult"), and certainly far from thinking of it as having anything to do with religion. Yet the very title refers to the silence, or absence, of God (the printed script's subtitle reads "God's silence: the negative impression"), an absence which seems to pervade the entire film.

The sisters Ester and Anna, and Anna's young son Johan, arrive by train in a strange city where an incomprehensible language is spoken and army tanks rumble menacingly and inexplicably through the streets. The weather is hot and oppressive. The visitors spend the night in a gloomy hotel with long, empty corridors, along which the boy aimlessly wanders. The two women are tormented in very different ways: the intellectual Ester, dying of a lung complaint, finds comfort in her radio and in solitude, while the sensual Anna frantically seeks fulfilment in casual sexual encounters. Both are wrapped up within themselves, and their inability to communicate leads to an argument which causes Anna and Johan to leave the city and Ester to die alone. As they leave, the boy reads some words of the foreign language which his aunt had written out for him, words for things like spirit, fear, and joy.

*The Silence* is clearly not a film for those seeking light entertainment or religious uplift; like many of Bergman's films it is tough going. But one must surely admire his technique in managing to create a powerful atmosphere which conveys absence and silence as positive attributes instead of as mere nothingness, a technique manifested in several ways.

There are for example the long-held shots, startling to viewers conditioned to the fast cutting of television and of most modern movies. In other contexts this can create an attitude of reverent contemplation (see for example *Ordet* and *The Sacrifice*), but here it contributes powerfully to an atmosphere which is calm yet threatening and oppressive.

Again, great care is taken with the soundtrack: there is no musical score (very unusual for a film), the train at the beginning is quite soundless, the hotel has a ghost-like silence. Along with Bresson and Tarkovsky, Bergman is one of the masters of the use of soundtrack to convey atmosphere. As always, Bergman's direction of actresses is superb.

The minimalist plot and location, the unexplained features like the tanks and the troupe of dwarfs who appear in the hotel, and the claustrophobic sets with their unrealistically bright lighting, all contribute to the general sense of oppression and unspecified threat.

Perhaps the key scene is where Anna, after being persistently questioned about her movements, revengefully lures Ester to witness her in the arms of a barman. Anna reminds her sister that, when their father died, Ester said she no longer wanted to live. "Why are you living still?" she devastatingly asks. For Ester her father's death was the death of God, and it is this chilling reminder that brings about her own death as the film ends.

*The Silence* has been described as a description of Hell on earth. It is a world where God is no more, and where as a consequence people have no reason for living. It is interesting that this view is being presented not by a Christian but by a man who had reached a near-atheistic position. Is Bergman saying that without God life is meaningless? It would seem so, from the evidence of this difficult and disturbing film.

## STALKER
## Andrei Tarkovsky, USSR, 1979

Based on a science-fiction story, *Roadside Picnic* by the Strugatsky brothers, *Stalker* was the fifth of Tarkovsky's seven feature films. The SF element is barely present in the film, however, which becomes a highly contemplative meditation upon religious faith, wrapped up in allegorical terms. It is not for those who like the crash-bang-wallop style of movie-making; for others it can be an intensely beautiful and rewarding experience, although patience is required.

The first quarter of the film is in monochrome. We are in the Stalker's house in a very decrepit industrial area. He is due to go and meet two other men, called Writer and Scientist, to act as guide in visiting a mysterious and dangerous area, probably radio-active, known as the Zone. Inside the Zone is a building containing the Room, whose function we discover later. Stalker's wife unsuccessfully pleads with him to stay with her and their crippled daughter. To reach the Zone the three men have to cross a border, complete with guards who fire on them; they get across on a railway-trolley. In a brilliant sequence the camera moves along parallel with the men (no tricks here with back-projection) and we see their heads in contemplative close-up, one by one, for a wordless three minutes or so, as the clanking of the wheels on the rails intermingles with electronic music. The effect is stunning.

Once in the Zone the photography becomes full colour. Stalker, the guide, throws metal nuts ahead of him to find the safe path, and the viewer has to sit patiently as the three men slowly make their way forward. This is a key feature of how *Stalker* is made; Tarkovsky makes "film" time approximate to "real" time, so that we are forced to experience the patience, and even perhaps the boredom, of the screen characters.

We learn that the Zone is a place where our most secret desire can be granted; not what we would like to *think* is our most secret wish, but what really is, within our heart of hearts. When the men reach the Room, Writer and Scientist dare not enter. They cannot face the reality of what is within them.

The period in the Zone contains some beautiful long-held shots involving water, a favourite *motif* of all Tarkovsky's films. In one shot we follow the course of a stream containing innumerable objects, both natural and man-made (including icons, which appear in one form or other in nearly all his films). In another shot, the final one before their return, the three men are sitting on the floor in a circle, when a sudden shower of rain lasting a minute or so pours down into a pool between them and the camera. Nothing is spoken; it is simply something that happens, and we respond to it as we wish, most naturally in a spirit of pure contemplation.

On returning to the squalid industrial landscape from which they started, when the three men have each, perhaps, gained something from their visit to the Zone, Stalker is reunited with his long-suffering devoted wife and his daughter who, it is hinted, may have been miraculously cured of being a cripple. But the real miracle is arguably the selfless love of Stalker's wife, who gives a powerful straight-to-camera monologue including the profoundly true words: "If there were no sorrow in life, it wouldn't be better, it would be worse!"

The character-type of Stalker is one common to most of Tarkovsky's films, a man who is weak in the world's eyes but determined to maintain his integrity, a "fool for Christ". A beautiful, enigmatic, and absorbing film, *Stalker* is ultimately saying not just that we should be in touch with our innermost selves, but also that love is the only thing that can make sense of the world. It repays repeated viewings.

# STROMBOLI
## Roberto Rossellini, Italy, 1949

The opening credits of this English-language movie, Rossellini's first of several starring Ingrid Bergman, reveal that there was a religious adviser, and this is followed on the screen by a quotation from Isaiah: "I have hearkened to those who have asked nothing of me. I have let myself be found by those who were not looking for me." Viewers may subsequently be puzzled by the minimal direct religious reference until the very end of the film, but this intensely moving ending provides a fully satisfying resolution and, to my mind, makes *Stromboli* one of the most underrated of all religious films. Some versions of the film have tampered with the ending in order to make it more "upbeat", but the ending described below is that intended by the director.

Ingrid Bergman plays Karin, a once-wealthy refugee in an Italian displaced persons' camp after the 1939-45 war. When her application for a visa is turned down she cynically resorts to accepting the marriage proposal of a poor fisherman as a means of escape. On arriving at Antonio's home on the volcanic island of Stromboli, however, she quickly realises the mistake she has made; there is nothing of the life she was used to, the conditions are primitive and harsh, nature is raw, her husband earns next to nothing, his English is little better than her Italian, and he has the traditional "macho" attitude of the Italian peasant. To make things worse the locals come to regard her as immodest, not least when she unwittingly visits a woman with a "bad reputation".

In a key scene Karin visits the local priest to seek help. She tells him that Antonio did not like the changes she has made in the house, and by use of her feminine charms tries to persuade him to give her some money so that she can escape. Rejecting her advances the priest makes it clear that her duty before God is to make a happy home and marriage for Antonio and herself. She storms out, shouting: "Your God won't help!"

When she is seen by some local women in an apparently compromising (but innocent) situation her reputation is further damaged, causing Antonio to beat her when he hears about it. In a long documentary-style section she goes with her husband to watch the tuna-fishing, and is sickened at the sight, obviously identifying her own position with that of the enormous but helpless fish.

After a volcanic eruption (which occurred in reality during filming) Karin tells Antonio that she has decided to go away, prompting him to imprison her in the house. She manages to get out, but discovers that her only means of escape from Stromboli is via the still-hot volcano to the village on the other side of the island. After climbing up she cries and sobs herself to sleep, but on waking she is overwhelmed by the beauty of the natural world around her. It is then that she has what, to me, is an utterly convincing religious experience, seeing God in the majesty of the still-smouldering volcano. Her final words, shouted to the winds, are: "God! My God! Help me! Give me the strength, the understanding, and the courage!" As the final image fades we still hear her "Oh God! Oh God!"

It is not clear whether she has decided to go back, and in a sense it does not matter; the question of whether she *should* do so is also unimportant for this purpose. She has come through a time of selfish motivation when she did not scruple to manipulate others to suit her needs, even to the extent of trying to seduce a priest, and has reached a stage of spirituality and of recognition of God's presence around her. *Stromboli* is a film which undoubtedly grows on one at a second or third viewing, with one of the most genuinely moving endings of all the films in this book.

# TEN COMMANDMENTS, THE
## Cecil B. DeMille, USA, 1956

A remake of DeMille's own 1923 silent epic, which in fact consisted largely of a modern story to which the Biblical part acted as prologue, this version of *The Ten Commandments*, DeMille's last film, is probably the best-known of all religious films. With a cast (people and animals) of literally tens of thousands, including a host of famous stars, stunning wide-screen special effects, and much location shooting, it is perhaps also the best-known epic movie, and if seen at all should undoubtedly be seen on the big screen.

The film is, more or less, the Biblical story of Moses, padded out with material from three novels and with an unwarranted love-interest thrown in for good measure. The Pharoah king hears that a Deliverer of the Hebrews will soon be born, and orders all newborn Hebrew males to be killed. The future Moses is spared by being sent downriver in a basket, to be found and brought up by Pharoah's sister. When Prince Moses (Charlton Heston), as he became, is grown up, Pharoah's son (Yul Brynner) is jealous of him, while the Princess Nefretiri openly (and fictitiously) lusts after him. Moses is banished when Pharoah discovers he has killed an Egyptian to save a Hebrew slave.

Years later, when Moses has discovered at the burning bush that he is the Deliverer appointed by God, he unsuccessfully urges Pharoah to set his people free. Moses brings forth the ten plagues of Egypt, and when Pharoah finally allows the Hebrews to go he sends his chariots after them. Moses raises his arms to divide the Red Sea for the Hebrews to cross, and when the Egyptians come after them they are drowned.

When Moses brings his people to Mount Sinai he climbs to the top to receive the stone tablets engraved with the Ten Commandments. When the

84

Hebrews build the Golden Calf Moses smashes the tablets against it, killing its worshippers. For forty years the Hebrews wander the desert before finding the Promised Land, and the film ends as Moses watches Joshua lead them across the Jordan.

For those familiar with the story of Moses, the main merit of *The Ten Commandments* is as spectacle rather than as education or religious inspiration. God manifests Himself through physical wonders rather than through the salvation of souls. The most famous scene is the parting of the Red Sea, an astonishing effect produced by photographing water pouring into a tank, reversing it, and superimposing on both images a shot of the people walking across. The 3-mile-long procession at the Exodus, chased by the specially-trained Egyptian army in their chariots, is almost as spectacular.

Charlton Heston's dignified and powerful performance was no doubt assisted by the intense seriousness with which he approached the part. Apparently he memorised great chunks of the Book of Exodus, insisted on doing many retakes of shots until he was satisfied, and even walked barefoot through the rocks of Mount Sinai just as Moses had done. DeMille later said that he chose Heston because of his resemblance to the Michaelangelo statue of Moses. Unfortunately much of the film's dialogue is spoken in the over-emphatic and ponderous manner one finds in "TV mini-series".

DeMille was a staunchly believing Christian who tried to translate some of the more visually spectacular Bible stories on to the screen, while taking the occasional liberty for commercial reasons. Commendably, he insisted on a certain reverence when he considered it appropriate; for example, in *The Ten Commandments* he refrained from making public the name of the actor who spoke the words of God to Moses. Basically, however, this film is a rattling good entertainment rather than a spiritual work of art.

# THROUGH A GLASS DARKLY
## Ingmar Bergman, Sweden, 1961

The first film of Bergman's early-1960s trilogy is concerned with his frequent themes of loneliness, non-communication, and a search for a God who may or may not be there. Like the other Bergman films covered in this book it represents a stage in the director's sincere and anguished probing after religious truth as he approached middle age.

Set in the island home of the widowed writer David, the film has only three other characters: David's son and daughter Minus and Karin, and Karin's husband Martin. David has immersed himself in his writing, dropping in *en route* from Switzerland to Yugoslavia to see the family he generally neglects. Karin is having a schizophrenic breakdown while Martin, unable to help her, engrosses himself in his work as a medical lecturer. The 17-year-old Minus is in the throes of adolescent sexuality.

In a key scene near the start of the film, the other three characters perform a play in honour of David's return. Minus portrays a poet who, for the sake of his art, refuses to accompany a princess (Karin) in her descent to the land of darkness. David is hurt by this implied but undoubted rebuke, but refuses to show it.

Karin's illness causes her to believe that God dwells behind the wallpaper, and she communes with Him through the cracks. Eventually she thinks she sees God in the form of a large spider, just as a spider-shaped helicopter arrives to take her away to hospital. David finally realises how he has put his third-rate art before his family, and tells Minus: "God is love. *Every* sort of love. The highest and the lowest, the poorest and the richest, the most ridiculous and the most sublime." He says that his hopes lie in knowing that love is real, though we cannot know whether love proves God's existence or whether love itself is God. "Daddy spoke to me!" is Minus' response to this breach of the communication barrier.

The film's treatment of David is a clear condemnation of the artist who sacrifices others for the sake of his vocation; indeed, in a revealing moment of possible self-criticism, Bergman has David put on the very type of garments (beret and leather jacket) which Bergman himself wore when filming. David's main problem is the gap between inspiration and articulation, a failure of language, hostile and alienating, which becomes a major theme of *The Silence*, the third film of the trilogy.

David's speech at the time of his final change of heart can perhaps be taken as a snapshot of Bergman's own attitude towards God at this time. Love is the highest of all values, especially when it involves sacrifice (as it invariably must). If this is how we define God, says Bergman, so be it. Love is something real, and it does not particularly matter whether God is objectively distinct from it. If He *is* distinct He is, perhaps, to be identified with the malignant spider-shaped helicopter who comes to fetch Karin.

Clearly this is far from a Christian viewpoint, and Bergman was by this time well on the road to the atheism which, to all intents and purposes, he came to embrace after *The Silence* (an attitude which was certainly strongly influenced by his upbringing under a stern and cruel Lutheran father). As I point out elsewhere, however, sincere atheism or agnosticism cannot and should not be simply ignored or wished away by Christians.

*Through A Glass Darkly* is not one of Bergman's greatest films, although the acting is, as always, superb, and the use of soundtrack (birds, footsteps, foghorns, rain, as well as Bach at a key moment) is exquisite. The film is probably best seen in the context of the whole trilogy, which is occasionally screened in repertory cinemas.

# TOKYO STORY
## Yasujiro Ozu, Japan, 1953

*Tokyo Story* may seem a strange choice for an anthology of religious films: an everyday tale of an ordinary Japanese family where the only religious reference is a short scene of a Buddhist funeral. I make no apology for its inclusion, however. In his book "Transcendental Style in Film" the American film writer Paul Schrader analyses Ozu's films in terms of their affinity with a major strand of Japanese painting, steeped in the Buddhist tradition of meditation and contemplation. The archetypal Ozu film, *Tokyo Story* is shot almost entirely from a low angle with barely a single camera movement, encouraging a contemplative and concentrated response from the viewer. This is combined with the highly unusual technique, here so unobtrusive that one barely notices, of having much of the dialogue spoken straight to camera. In addition sequences are separated not by fades or dissolves but by simple shots of the world outside, such as rooftops or boats chug-chugging on the river; the world goes on, whatever is happening to particular individuals. Because the subject-matter is concerned with some of the deepest and most universal human emotions and experiences, the viewer is drawn so totally into the lives of these ordinary people that the film becomes unbearably and authentically moving, without a trace of the sentimentality and over-acting normally associated with films dealing with family tragedy.

An elderly couple, the Hirayamas, take the train to Tokyo to visit their married children, the doctor son Koichi and beautician daughter Shige. Another daughter, Kyoko, remains at home, while a son lives in a different town. Not long after arriving they begin to realise that their children are not particularly overjoyed to see them, being too busy with their jobs, while their two grandsons are spoilt and show no interest in them. However their daughter-in-law Noriko, the widow of a son who died in the war, takes far more trouble over them, having time off work to show them round.

On arriving back home Mrs. Hirayama falls very ill, and her four children and Noriko gather around the bedside. The old lady dies, and after the funeral the last person to leave for home is Noriko.

Ozu is regarded as the most "traditional" of Japanese directors, in both subject and style. In *Tokyo Story* he portrays what he obviously felt strongly about, the breakdown of the Japanese family and the rejection of their parents by people in pursuit of material rewards. So masterfully is this portrayed that these characters come to be almost our own family, and it is easy to become unaware that it is all in Japanese and that we are reading sub-titles.

Ozu is known to have been a stern taskmaster with his actors, shooting scenes many times over until he had exactly the effect he wanted. This certainly pays off; there are many little added touches and bits of dialogue which help to make the film the masterpiece it undoubtedly is. It is impossible to remain dry-eyed when, after the mother's death, Kyoko says to Noriko: "Isn't life disappointing?" to which the gently smiling reply is "I'm afraid it is"; or when Noriko breaks down when the old man gives her his dead wife's watch (described by Paul Schrader as the moment of "stasis").

Noriko, played by Setsuko Hara, is surely one of the most supremely good and lovely characters ever portrayed on film. Selfless, modest, uncomplaining, and realistic without being cynical, she is what Christians would call a living saint. Yet there is no sense in which she is somehow "superhuman", often a fault of screen portrayals of admirable people. She is simply a model which ordinary people can seek to emulate.

## TRIAL OF JOAN OF ARC, THE
## Robert Bresson, France, 1961

Apart from Carl Dreyer's silent classic *The Passion of Joan of Arc*, Bresson's is the best of the many films about the Maid of Orléans. Based strictly on extracts from the official transcripts of the trial, it can claim to be of real historical and academic interest, as well as incorporating Bresson's usual pared-down asceticism, monotonic expressionless acting, and a highly rhythmic structure which enables the viewer almost to *feel* what is going on below the surface. Far from being an historical reconstruction, it is more an attempt to portray the *essence* of the trial and its characters. Although only 65 minutes long, such is the pace of the dialogue that it can leave the viewer feeling mentally exhausted.

After a brief pre-credits sequence showing Joan's rehabilitation some years after her death, most of the film consists of a series of nine interrogations, some in the trial room and some, apparently illegal, in her cell. These alternating locations, linked by shots of soldiers going up and down the stone steps in the tower, are part of the rhythmic structure referred to above. Within the scenes there is the rhythm of question-and-answer and the corresponding cutting back and forth between Joan and her examiners, the rhythm of the English voices (Burn the witch!) acting as a sort of counterpoint to the French ones, and the natural sounds like the clanking of chains, the opening and closing of heavy doors, and the scratching of pens during the interrogations. This is all very deliberate; Bresson explained in a magazine interview that he imposed a very rapid rhythm on the film because of the slowness of the trial itself.

Each of the nine interrogations covers broadly the same ground, and Bresson, who wrote the screenplay, selected those extracts which enable

Joan to reveal a little more about herself each time, showing the viewer her interior struggle. This emphasis on words, a particular feature of this film, might seem to some to negate the function of cinema, but it is still intensely visual. Most of it is shot from Joan's own point of view, and we generally see only a small part of the location; we never see the whole courtroom, for example. There is also the crucial element of the unspoken; looks and gestures speak volumes, while the wordless scene where Joan's virginity is verified in her cell consists simply of three women who turn to the camera and move out of the frame, as Joan pulls the sheet over her up to her eyes.

The final scene of the execution is superb. Whereas throughout the trial Joan has been in chains, every movement of her feet being accompanied by clanking, now she is free of them and we see her bare feet, restricted by her shift, almost *scampering* to the stake. Once on the scaffold, symbolic bright sunlight shines directly on her face. As the flames start to rise and crackle, the crowd, whom we hear rather than see, falls silent. Two monks hold out a large cross before her. Joan cries out that all her revelations were from God, and then, completely hidden by the smoke, she calls "Jesus!". Shots of a dog and some pigeons show us that ordinary life goes on despite the drama. The smoke clears, and we see the empty stake, pointing towards heaven. By implication, that is where Joan has gone.

The film has been criticised by some on the grounds of Florence Carrez' performance as Joan: too insipid, no sense of spiritual struggle. I cannot agree. A non-professional who did precisely as she was instructed, her struggle is conveyed in the selection of verbal extracts from the trial, and the very impassivity of her delivery enables us to "see" more than just the outward appearance. *The Trial of Joan of Arc* is one of the most remarkable of all religious films.

# UNDER SATAN'S SUN
## Maurice Pialat, France, 1987

The novels of the French Catholic writer
Georges Bernanos are usually associated with his co-
religionist compatriot Robert Bresson, who based
*Diary of a Country Priest* and *Mouchette* on two of
his books. More recently Bernanos' first novel, *Sous
le Soleil de Satan*, has been brought to the screen
by the self-professed atheist Maurice Pialat, and it
provides an interesting contrast with the Bresson
films. The more conventional Pialat uses
professional actors and eschews the other's extreme
austerity of image, while retaining something of the
fast expressionless style of delivery common to
Bresson's characters.

Set in turn-of-the-century rural France, the
film tells of Father Donissan who, feeling himself a
failure to his village flock, urges his Dean to send
him away somewhere. The worldly-minded Dean,
admiring the self-flagellating Donissan's saintliness
and intense awareness of the power of evil,
persuades him to stay on.

In an important sub-plot one of Donissan's
parishioners, the beautiful 16-year-old Mouchette, is
expecting a child by the local Deputy (M.P.) Gallet.
After saying she wants to move in with him, and
telling him that her father has beaten a confession
out of her, she shoots him with his own shotgun in
such a way as to make it look like suicide.
Visiting her other lover, the young doctor Cadignan,
she accuses him of being the father of her child and
describes how she killed Gallet. He disbelieves both
stories.

Walking to another parish by night, Donissan
meets up with a horse-dealer. When the priest
stumbles and falls the man gently kisses him,
saying: "I kiss you all, you bear me in your flesh."
Recognising him to be Satan, Donissan refuses his
temptation, namely of knowing people's innermost

thoughts. Nevertheless he is now possessed of this frightening gift.

When he meets Mouchette he knows that she killed Gallet, and absolves her. At home later she kills herself; when Donissan carries her body to the church to pray for a resurrection, his superiors are scandalised and he is sent to a monastery.

Several years later Father Donissan has become venerated almost as a saint in the parish of Lumbres. Called to the bedside of a boy dying of meningitis he unsuccessfully tries to restore him to life. Returning to the church, he suffers a heart attack and himself dies in the confessional.

Although an atheist, the director clearly had no intention of turning Bernanos' novel into an anti-religious tract, although the film's notable absence of simple Christian joy might be taken as evidence of selective interpretation. Pialat, whose films generally exhibit a bleak pessimism, seems fascinated by the source material, and by the idea of the embodiment of sin and evil in the concrete, such as the horse-dealer; the director cast himself as Donissan's Dean. The priest-hero is played by the ubiquitous Gérard Depardieu, best-known in Britain as Jean de Florette, and the versatile actor solemnly shambles his way through the film with utter conviction, a character absolutely honest if of somewhat limited charisma, despite his veneration by the parishioners of Lumbres.

The character of Father Donissan, with his ability to read people's souls, has had famous real-life counterparts in the Curé d'Ars and Padre Pio. The difference, however, is that Bernanos' character receives his gift from the Devil, which is why he is so reluctant to use it. Some may find the whole idea of a story based on this supposition distasteful. For others, *Under Satan's Sun* is an interesting, if somewhat gloomy, portrayal of the powers of incarnate evil in a rural Christian setting.

# VIRGIN SPRING, THE
Ingmar Bergman, Sweden, 1959

Like *The Seventh Seal*, *The Virgin Spring* is a medieval parable containing some violent scenes. From a religious point of view, however, it is perhaps the most positive of all Bergman's films, symbolising the age-old conflict between Good and Evil.

Based on a 14th century legend, the film tells of an upright Christian husband, Töre, who shares mutual affection with his beautiful but spoilt daughter Karin. Karin's half-sister Ingeri is jealous of her, and when the two are to set out by horse on the long journey to church Ingeri puts a toad in the other's bread, and curses her in the name of the Nordic god Odin.

As the two girls ride to church, Ingeri comes to realise the evil she has unleashed, and refuses to enter the forest. Instead she visits an old man who tells her of "three dead men riding north". As Karin proceeds alone she is spied by three goatherds, one just a boy, who dash to intercept her. After some playful banter, the toad placed in the bread suddenly appears, causing Karin, in attempting to flee, to become caught in a tree. The three herdsmen then violate her in turn, and one strikes her dead. The young boy, left on guard by the other two, covers her body with earth. All has been watched by the horrified Ingeri.

The unsuspecting three seek shelter for the night at Töre's house. When Töre discovers what the three have done his desire for vengeance knows no bounds. After uprooting a birch tree and flagellating himself with it, he stabs one man through the heart, crushes the other in a fire, and flings the boy against the wall.

When Töre and his wife find Karin's body he is smitten with remorse, and with his eyes to heaven utters: "I don't understand you, God. Yet I ask for forgiveness, for I know of no other way to live." He vows to build a church in penance for his sin. As they lift the dead Karin's head for the second .time, a spring now gushes from the spot, a direct response to his vow. This miracle is the most positively Christian moment in all Bergman's films. Finally, Ingeri bathes her face in the stream, exorcising the evil she brought about through her curse.

The stark conflict between Good and Evil, portrayed in the film, seems to be felt particularly keenly by Bergman. He has said: "Our whole existence is based on the fact that there are things we may do and others we may not do, and these are the complications that we uninterruptedly, constantly come into contact with throughout our life." It goes without saying that it is one thing merely to be aware of God's laws, quite another to avoid the difficulties and complex situations which inevitably arise in trying to carry them out. Töre's killing of the three is clearly wrong and cannot be condoned, but how many of us would not react that way in that situation if we had the opportunity? To Töre's credit he deeply repents of his act.

The Good-Evil dichotomy is evident not just in the immorality of the rape and murders, but also in the battle between Christianity and paganism portrayed by Ingeri's curse. Her repentance of this is as significant and deeply-felt as her father's repentance of *his* deeds. In our own day the invoking of pagan gods would raise barely an eyebrow; the modern concept of "wrongdoing" has been reduced to little more than the infliction of physical pain or material loss to others.

*The Virgin Spring* is generally regarded as one of Bergman's lesser films, although the cinematography is splendid and Max von Sydow as Töre is excellent. The Christian themes of Good and Evil, repentance, forgiveness, and miracle make it a meaty offering for anyone interested in the serious treatment of religion in the cinema.

# VIRIDIANA
## Luis Buñuel, Spain, 1961

As noted earlier, there are certainly many
people for whom Buñuel's films would not be found
acceptable. He attacks what he sees as bourgeois
morality and its institutions, including the Church,
with a wicked glee, and *Viridiana* is one of his two
films containing scenes of alleged blasphemy (the
other being *L'Age d'Or*). My view, however, is that
sincere and informed attacks on aspects of Christian
practice should be faced and even welcomed, as they
may well be pointing out a perversion which can be
corrected.

Viridiana is an idealistic young nun about to
take her final vows. Her superior urges her to
visit her wealthy uncle by marriage, Don Jaime, who
has been supporting her. She does so, determined to
eschew the luxuries at the estate. Don Jaime is
extremely kind and polite, but is secretly besotted
with his niece's resemblance to his wife who died 30
years ago on their wedding night. After drugging
her and unsuccessfully trying to seduce her, he tells
her that she cannot return to the convent as she has
lost her virginity. At this she rushes off, causing
the obviously mentally-sick man to kill himself.

On hearing of her uncle's suicide Viridiana
decides that her future lies not in the convent but
back on the estate, of which she is now part-owner
along with Don Jaime's illegitimate son Jorge,
helping the neediest in society. Gathering together
a motley collection of down-and-outs, she agrees to
feed and house them in return for their doing some
chores. The outcasts take full advantage of the
situation, doing as little as possible and fighting
among themselves.

When Viridiana and Jorge are away on business,
the outcasts break into the house and treat
themselves to a riotous feast. At one point, to the
sound of the *Hallelujah Chorus* blaring from a

gramophone, a woman pretends to photograph the men as they are seated at a long table in the positions of Christ and the disciples as portrayed in Leonardo's *Last Supper*; this is the scene which provoked accusations of blasphemy. Viridiana and Jorge return to a scene of chaos, and the young nun's illusions are totally shattered.

The Church is just one of several targets. Others are idealism and humanitarian liberalism, both illustrated in this film. Viridiana is portrayed as an idealist who thinks that good intentions are enough to bring about the improvement and well-being of people, and who simply does not understand that the outcasts will not respond in the way she expects. Jorge is a more practical person who at least gets some useful things done around the estate, but the inadequacy of his liberalism is illustrated in a scene where he frees a dog tied to a moving wagon, only for another wagon, with another captive dog, to pass in the opposite direction. A Christian would say that one little act of kindness is good and valuable in itself; Buñuel seems to be saying that it is but a drop in the ocean, so why not just be a cynic?

*Viridiana* is not for the sensitive; it is for those who can withstand, and perhaps enjoy and even learn from, a witty attack on their values. It is also, of course, for those who share Buñuel's attitudes anyway!

And what about the blasphemy? There are differing views on this, but for me blasphemy, like beauty, is largely in the eye of the beholder. I would certainly object to insulting portrayals of, or derogatory comments about, any central figure of the Christian religion, but to parody a famous painting is surely not in the same league as this. So for me *Viridiana* is not objectionable, although I would not wish those who might be offended to see it, nor do I insist that somebody has to have seen a film before objecting to it.

# VOYAGE TO ITALY
## Roberto Rossellini, Italy, 1953

Known also under such titles as *Journey to Italy* and *The Lonely Woman*, not to mention its Italian title *Viaggio in Italia*, this English-language movie is a strikingly original example of a highly spiritual film which on the surface has little to do with religion. It is basically about the effect of a new environment, which can be seen as a metaphor for God, on the interior state of the characters. The film is virtually plotless, and it is known that the two stars, Ingrid Bergman and George Sanders, were particularly ill-at-ease while making it. This adds to, rather than detracts from, their performances, and indicates Rossellini's skill as one of the greatest directors.

Alexander and Katherine Joyce are an English couple arriving in Naples to arrange the selling of Alexander's late uncle's house. Their conversation tells us that their marriage is not a happy one, and that Alexander finds Italy a boring and irritating country. The state of their marriage is contrasted with that of the Burtons with whom they have arranged to stay, and the happiness of this couple provokes memories in Katherine of her one-time love for a poet who died very young.

During the daytime the two go their separate ways. Katherine visits the Archaeological Museum in Naples, where a very old guide shows her the Greek statues housed there. The emphasis in this sequence is on Katherine's reactions, mostly the shocked surprise of a reserved Englishwoman at the sensuality of this ancient culture. On another occasion she visits the catacombs of a church with Mrs. Burton, and is shaken by seeing the piles of skulls.

The evening social occasions which the couple have to attend lead only to recriminations. Alexander's attentiveness to other women at a restaurant occasions an angry outburst from his wife, but the tables are turned when Katherine appears to respond to male flirtatiousness at a party. When Katherine leaves Alexander without their car, he uses this trivial incident as an excuse to ask her for a divorce.

In the final section of the film the couple visit the ruins of Pompeii, and are deeply impressed when a perfectly-preserved couple are dug out of the solid lava. Totally overcome by the experience Katherine suddenly demands to be taken home, but as they try to drive back to the Burtons they become caught up in the famous St. Januarius procession where the saint's blood is supposed to liquify on certain dates. Unable to proceed they get out of their car, but become separated by the mass of people. At that moment, as voices in the crowd are proclaiming a miracle and a man is seen waving crutches, they suddenly realise their mutual need.

The meaning of the film's ending is obvious: two miracles, the one (if it is one) in a crudely physical, wonder-working sense, the other the seemingly impossible reconciliation of two estranged human beings. It is the rest of the film which presents difficulties to some viewers. What is the point of Ingrid Bergman spending ages wandering around museums and through catacombs, and of the scenes at Pompeii? It is surely that the environment of the area, totally unlike what the Joyces are used to, is working on their hearts and minds to open them to a reconciliation, like the grace of God working through people. The effect is deepened by the emphasis on old age, death, and decay (Katherine's remark at Pompeii that "life is so short" is deeply moving) as well as on vitality (the sensuous statues) and new birth (the many babies and pregnant women she sees in Naples). *Voyage to Italy* is a film which may at first be puzzling, but which undoubtedly becomes far more impressive, almost hypnotically so, on subsequent viewings.

# WHISTLE DOWN THE WIND
## Bryan Forbes, GB, 1961

A film which is clearly an allegory, *Whistle Down the Wind* largely avoids the mawkishness and sentimentality which can so easily afflict this type of material. Adapted from a novel by Mary Hayley Bell, whose daughter Hayley Mills stars, it involved a plethora of well-known British names: Alan Bates and Bernard Lee in leading rôles, Richard Attenborough as producer, Keith Waterhouse and Willis Hall as writers, and Malcolm Arnold writing the atmospheric musical score.

It tells of three motherless children with a strict religious upbringing, living on a Lancashire farm, who save some kittens from drowning and decide to hide them in a barn. There they find a wild-eyed bearded man with a gun, and on being asked who he is he replies "Jesus Christ!" As the older girl has previously been told by a Salvation Army woman that Jesus would keep the kittens from harm, the children take the man's answer at face value.

The man is in fact a murderer on the run, but the news of Christ's second coming quickly spreads among the village children, who bring him gifts in order to keep on the right side of him. The children fear that Jesus will be taken away as he was once before, so they keep the adults in the dark until the younger girl blurts it out at a party. The police are called, but the man has been so mellowed by the children, or else so moved that he does not wish to betray their faith in him, that he surrenders himself without trying to shoot his way out. As he is taken away two of the children arrive, and the elder girl says to the boy: "You missed him this time, but he'll come again." The 6-year-old boy, however, ceased to believe when one of the kittens died: "That's not Jesus, that's just a feller."

The film contains some obvious Gospel references: the boy who, under threat, betrays the secret three times to the local bully, or the way the man stretches out his arms as if on a cross as the police search him. Such scenes are not laid on heavily, however, and the children's practical and matter-of-fact attitude throughout keeps the film's feet firmly on the ground; one suspects that Hollywood would have approached this material in a very different way. The early scenes help to prepare the children's minds for the encounter, so that their acceptance of the man's supposed identity seems perfectly natural in context.

Jesus said that unless we come to him as little children, we shall not enter the Kingdom of Heaven. This means that we are to be childlike (not child*ish*) in our approach, maintaining an attitude of openness and wonder to the world. This is something we inevitably lose, at least in part, as we become adult and are exposed to the cynicism and cruelty of the so-called "real" world. How true it is that each time we suffer an injustice, whether real or imagined, we become harder and more defensive; selfish and wrong acts lead to greater selfishness in others, which spreads throughout society like a cancer. The reverse is also true, as is illustrated in this film; the children's effect on the man causes him to give himself up without a fight, perhaps as a sign of sincere repentance.

It is regrettable that the period of childlike innocence in youngsters' lives seems to have become progressively shorter in recent times. In 1961 it did not seem strange that a girl of the age of the Hayley Mills character should believe that the man was Jesus. Her counterpart 30 years later, brought up on a diet of seedy TV soaps and pornographic comics which pass for "newspapers" in many British homes, prides herself on being "streetwise". Sadly, *Whistle Down the Wind* seems very dated, a fault not of the film but of society.

# WILD STRAWBERRIES
## Ingmar Bergman, Sweden, 1957

Arguably Bergman's most finely constructed film, *Wild Strawberries* is a superb "road movie" long before that term came into use. Like several of the Swedish master's movies it contains some semi-autobiographical elements. It is a meditation upon memory, old age, and death, and if this sounds depressing there are some delightfully light moments to offset the main theme.

The film covers a 24-hour period in the life of the 76-year-old professor Isak Borg (are the initials deliberate?) who travels from his Stockholm home to Lund to receive an honorary degree. Parallel with this physical journey is a semi-spiritual odyssey in which, through dreams and recollections, he comes to understand that his selfish withdrawal from the concerns of those around him is not the attitude of a mature human being.

Almost at the start of the film is a famous nightmare sequence when Isak, alone in a brilliantly-sunlit but empty street, sees a clock with no hands, a man with no face, and a horse-drawn hearse whose coffin falls open to reveal Borg himself. (Bergman himself is said to have had this dream several times.) Isak awakes on the day of his journey, to be undertaken by car with his daughter-in-law Marianne. The scenes of the journey, during which we discover that Isak is a rather selfish person who does not enjoy particularly good relations with others, are interspersed with more dreams, memories, visits, and other events, which help him to reach a greater degree of self-knowledge.

One of the key scenes is when they stop at the lakeside house where he lived long ago. Finding some wild strawberries, symbolising renewal of life, Isak is transported back through time to see his beautiful cousin and fiancée Sara, who was to reject him and marry his brother. Following her into the house he sees the whole family of his youth, although he is invisible to them.

Shortly afterwards on the journey they meet a trio of hitchhikers: two young men who engage in fierce theological arguments (presumably representing Bergman's own internal religious conflicts) and a girl called Sara who strikingly resembles his cousin. There is also an accident with a quarrelsome married couple in another car; Isak agrees to give them a lift until Marianne turns them out when their mutual bitterness becomes unbearable. Rather unfairly perhaps, the couple are portrayed as Catholics.

On the way Isak visits the somewhat deathly figure of his 96-year-old mother, calls in at a garage where the attendant knows him, and falls asleep again to dream of being academically humiliated at the hands of an examiner and being shown his long-dead wife in the arms of another man. Later Marianne recounts to him how her husband Evald (Isak's son) had refused to bring a child into the world because he was the product of an unhappy marriage.

The award of Isak's degree, which is filmed at Lund Cathedral, goes off perfectly, and there is a heartwarming scene that evening when the three young hitchhikers serenade Isak below his bedroom window. In the beautiful final scene Isak has a vision of being led by his cousin Sara to see his own parents, when young, sitting by the shore; this sends him to sleep in peace.

All these experiences have helped Isak to become less egotistical and more compassionate and peaceful. As in all Bergman films the performances are splendid, especially that of the veteran actor and director Victor Sjöstrom as Isak. This ultimately optimistic film, concerning itself with some of the deepest questions of human life, is one of the cinema's masterworks.

# WINTER LIGHT
## Ingmar Bergman, Sweden, 1962

The middle film of Bergman's trilogy of the early 1960s, *Winter Light* (sometimes known as *The Communicants*) portrays the loss of faith of the widowed pastor Tomas as he goes about his religious duties one cold winter's day. Needless to say, this utterly bleak but absorbing film can be taken as representing the director's own spiritual state of mind at the time.

As the film opens, Tomas is conducting a midday communion service in a neighbouring village church before a small congregation, which includes the schoolteacher Märta who loves him, the eccentric fisherman Jonas, and the crippled sexton Algot. After the service Jonas comes to Tomas to express his fears about the Chinese having the atomic bomb, fears which Tomas cannot or will not allay. Unable to shake himself free of his wife's memory, Tomas violently refuses marriage to Märta. Later he is shocked to learn that Jonas has killed himself. As the cold Swedish night envelops Tomas' own little church at just 3 p.m. the disillusioned pastor, now in a state of total spiritual sterility, prepares to conduct Evensong, with just Märta and Algot in attendance.

*Winter Light* can be seen as a sort of Passion of Tomas, his Way of the Cross as he moves from doubt to despair in what he comes to realise is, for him, a meaningless ritual; alone in his church he cries out: "God, my God, why have you abandoned me?". The events of the three hours, particularly the suicide of Jonas, bring home to the pastor the truth of his state.

Märta is an atheist, seeing human relationships as the most important thing in life. However, her desire to sacrifice herself for Tomas, her willingness to accept his brusque rejection, and even her eczema, mark her out as a sort of Christ-figure.

104